To:

From:

Date:

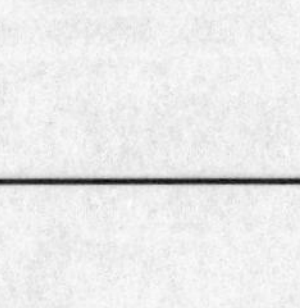

OUR VISION

The objective of our mission is to spiritually feed God's people through preaching and teaching and to take the Word of God everywhere it is needed.

ISBN: 1-59272-023-4

First Edition 2004

Cover designed by:
GM International - Design Department

Interior Design by:
GM International

Bible verses taken from:
New King James Version © 1982 by Thomas Nelson, Inc.

Category:
Spiritual Leadership

Printed by:
GM Munistries

Impreso en Colombia
Printed in Colombia

Leaders that Conquer

Leaders that Conquer

Men and women that will impact the world in this century

Guillermo Maldonado

GM MINISTRIES

Dedication

I dedicate this book to the men and women that want to make a difference in this world, to those who keep going regardless of the obstacles and who aspire to become what God planned for them to be, leaders that conquer.

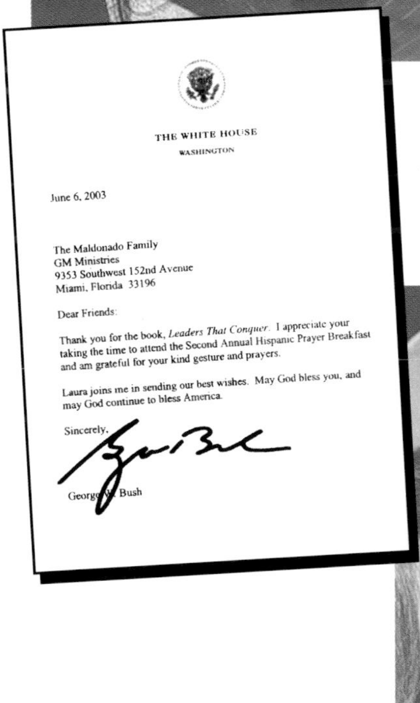

THE WHITE HOUSE
WASHINGTON

June 6, 2003

The Maldonado Family
GM Ministries
9353 Southwest 152nd Avenue
Miami, Florida 33196

Dear Friends:

Thank you for the book, *Leaders That Conquer*. I appreciate your taking the time to attend the Second Annual Hispanic Prayer Breakfast and am grateful for your kind gesture and prayers.

Laura joins me in sending our best wishes. May God bless you, and may God continue to bless America.

Sincerely,

George W. Bush

Pastor Guillermo Maldonado gives the President of the United States, George W. Bush, his book, ***Leaders that Conquer***, during the ***2003 National Hispanic Prayer Breakfast***, which took place on May 15, 2003, at the Capital Hilton, Washington, DC.

Pastor Guillermo Maldonado gives the President of the Dominican Republic, Hipolito Mejia, his books, ***Leaders that Conquer*** and ***Prayer***, on August 28, 2003, at the National Palace in Santo Domingo, Dominican Republic.

Acknowledgements

I am thankful to God for His grace upon my family, ministry and me. I would also like to express my appreciation and acknowledge the people that, contribute daily, in the development of this ministry. May God fill them with His grace and favor.

Index

Foreword

Seldom do I pick up a book that bowls me over. This book *Leaders that Conquer* literally rocked my world! Guillermo Maldonado's clarity, simplicity and practical advice made this book become my most recommended for leadership. I often found myself saying, "That's so simple – Why didn't I think of that?" This book is filled with just those kinds of insightful solutions. You won't just read this book; you will keep it handy for quick reference. In fact, I don't think you'll even let people borrow your copy! The section of the book that teaches you how to deal with difficult people is especially helpful. I also liked the portion on mentoring. You will be impacted by such statements as "No man is totally accepted until he has been totally rejected."

As you can tell by my prejudicial cheerleading – <u>I like this book</u> – and I also think you'll like this book. I like the book, and I love the man! Guillermo Maldonado is an anointed apostolic leader. Let him share with you the lessons he has learned. Tuition in life is cheaper when taught than experienced. You can learn life lessons from the book *Leaders that Conquer*. Oh …. And by the way, don't ask to borrow my copy!

Tommy Tenney
God Chasers Network

Commentaries

Guillermo Maldonado proves the written revelations throughout this book to be true and manageable. He has built up a church with thousands of saints; the majority of whom are leaders. As we read this book, we will be edified, transformed and perfected to become completely qualified leaders.

Every leader should take hold of the biblical principles for leadership presented in this book. When we learn to understand the ingredients that make up great leaders, then we will become the leaders God desires us to be.

Guillermo teaches us through Scripture, and in detail, how to confront effectively. One of the most important keys presented in this book is the ability to develop discipleship and to delegate authority and responsibility to others. To become effective leaders we must have our priorities in order and practice high levels of excellence. We'll also realize there is a high price to pay to become great leaders for God's people. Nonetheless, the attributes we receive and the rewards from God make this invested time, effort and commitment worthwhile, as we become the kind of leader God wants us to be.

Bill Hamon, Apostle and Bishop
Christian International Ministries Network

Once again, a tool that covers a very important subject is made available to the Church.

Leaders that Conquer by the Apostle Guillermo Maldonado, should be required reading for active pastors and leaders, as well as future ones.

The teachings of Jesus, *"...apart from Me you can do nothing,"* is the God-dependent theme that runs like a golden thread through the comprehensive spectrum of requirements, qualifications and expectations of a leader. It begins with that which is basic and builds toward a completed work of spirit, soul, mind and body.

The devotional life of a leader is specially founded on principles that express proper priorities that must be achieved. In this book, we find abundant definitions, lists, explanations, examples and commentaries.

The Apostle and Pastor Guillermo Maldonado has been promoted by God to a place of great responsibility, of administering and ministering to the physical and spiritual welfare of the fastest and largest growing Hispanic church in Florida. I strongly endorse this work and wholeheartily believe it will enhance and be an important tool to your spiritual, emotional and physical life as a servant and Son of God.

Apostle and Teacher to the Hispanic World
Dr. Ronald E. Short

One of John Maxwell's most repeated axioms is: *Everything stands or falls on leadership. I* agree with this. My 35 years of researching, teaching, and writing on church growth continually shows me that pastors who are leaders are the ones most strongly impacting their cities and regions for the kingdom of God.

It should go without saying that not all pastors are leaders. This is confirmed by the fact that ninety percent of American churches have 200 members or less. Almost any pastor or pastor-teacher can take a church up to the 200 barrier. Leadership skills may be helpful to move a church toward the upper parts of this range, but other factors such as location, parishoners' attitudes, worship quality, stimulating teaching, spiritual power in healing and deliverance, facilities, church traditions, and things like that help determine the size of the church as well. In other words, leadership is not particularly necessary to get a church up to 200 members. Moving beyond 200 is another story. A church will not grow steadily past 200 without leadership. The eight or nine percent of American churches in the 200-700/800 range have senior pastors who are leaders, to say nothing of the one to two percent numbering members in the thousands such as El Rey Jesús Church pastored by the author of this book, Guillermo Maldonado.

I have known Guillermo for many years, and every time I visit his work in Miami. I am once again amazed at the incredible exploits that God continually does through him. I have met few leaders whom I respect more than Pastor Maldonado. Not only does he have the spiritual gift of leadership, but God has also entrusted him with the gift of apostleship. Among other things, Guillermo takes very seriously his apostolic responsibility to "equip the saints for the work of the ministry" (see Eph. 4:12).

That is why he wrote this book, *Leaders That Conquer.* He wants to equip you for moving to a level of effectiveness in your ministry, whether in the church or in the workplace, that you might have desired but have yet to attain. In my library, I have an entire shelf of books on leadership. *Leaders That Conquer* ranks right up there with the best of them. In fact, from now on when someone asks me, "Which book on leadership would you most recommend?" I will say, "*Leaders That Conquer.*" I'm sure that when you read this book you will agree with me.

C. Peter Wagner, Presiding Apostle
International Coalition of Apostles

Chaos and delay best describe the home or organization absent of leadership, while order and progress typify its presence. Civilization, as we know it today, would not have evolved without leaders and plans. God knew this in His infinite wisdom and established leadership at the time of creation, giving Adam dominion over all of the earth and every living creature (Genesis 1:26). As you can see, the foundational pillars of structure and supervision have been essential to mankind since the inception of time.

When we turn on our televisions, we sometimes witness the shocking results due to the lack of leadership around the world. Lives are lost in vain, good causes are hindered and nations are torn apart. Man without guidance and control can be likened to a fish out of water, struggling to survive. We can be detrimental to others and even ourselves if we don't permit leadership to have its proper place in our lives. It was never intended for man to function outside the scope of leaders, whose much needed direction and setting of boundaries enables mankind to make a true difference in society. Submitting to leadership and purposing to be leaders ourselves not only equips us to impact the lives of others, but also aids us in becoming everything God intended us to be!

You could possible say that we were born to be leaders. Scripture states that we were made in the image of God, the ultimate leader. As such, I believe the seed of leadership exists within each of us, but we must make a conscious effort to discover that seed and nurture it for the Master's use. In his book, *Leaders that Conquer*, Dr. Guillermo Maldonado tells us the how and what of effective leadership. He candidly and profoundly shares the principles that are essential to the making of a "true" leader. If you desire to lead in the power and anointing of the Master, *Leaders that Conquer* is a book you must read. It will change your perspective on leadership and provide you with principles that will prepare you to be the best leader you can be – one that conquers!

Dr. Kingsley A. Fletcher
International Speaker, Author and Pastor
Research Triangle Park, NC

that we were made in the image of God, the ultimate leader. As such, I believe the seed of leadership exists within each of us, but we must make a conscious effort to discover that seed and nurture it for the Master's use. In his book, *Leaders that Conquer*, Dr. Guillermo Maldonado tells us the how and what of effective leadership. He candidly and profoundly shares the principles that are essential to the making of a "true" leader. If you desire to lead in the power and anointing of the Master, *Leaders that Conquer* is a book you must read. It will change your perspective on leadership and provide you with principles that will prepare you to be the best leader you can be—one that conquers!

Dr. Kingsley A. Fletcher
International Speaker, Author and Pastor
Research Triangle Park, NC

Introduction

Have you ever wondered why the world seems to be heading nowhere? Why men are unable to find their destiny, but simply follow the crowd from one place to another? We know that the answer to the first question is because Jesus is not in their hearts. However, if we study the life of Jesus in more detail, we will understand the reason for His teaching was for all mankind to re-discover their ability to be leaders and execute the original plan for their lives. This way, they will have lordship over God's creation.

I invite you to take an emotional journey through the pages of this book. It will help you to understand and develop the leadership potential within you, just as God designed it.

Leaders that Conquer is a book that will take you from God's original plan for man, to the uncontainable desire to fulfill His divine plan as God's leaders on earth. It is a strength that will change you from being ordinary and transform you into a unique person in the hands of the Creator. It helps you challenge what is established and prevents you from becoming comfortable with the way things are. You will learn to overcome every obstacle and limitation in such a way that it will change you in a way that will affect the lives of everyone around you. Furthermore, you will be an inspiration and motivator for those who come after you, seeking to fulfill their own destinies in God.

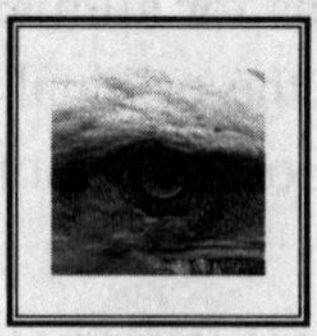

Chapter I

Developing Your Potential

The world is full of followers, supervisors and employers, but very few leaders. God created man with the potential to become leaders, but unfortunately, many go to their graves with their potentials undeveloped. Throughout their lives they were followers, never ascending to their God-Given leadership potential. However, many did leave their legacy here on earth. These people were men and women, prosperous and impoverished; they came from different cultures, colors and languages from around the world. They were simple and ordinary people who made the decision to make a difference and impact the world in different areas. Leaders are common people placed in extraordinary circumstances that force them to develop their potential and thus turning them into leaders. The world is in desperate need of leaders willing to stand up and inspire others to follow and fulfill the purpose and destiny of God for their lives. A good leader knows where he is going and inspires others to follow him. Every person has the God-given potential to become a leader, yet not all achieve their potential.

Before studying what potential is, we first must analyze its definition.

What is the meaning of the word "potential"?

It is something powerful, lying dormant within us, something of great power that has yet to come into existence or life, it exists only in possibilities, but not in reality. We must keep in mind the synonyms for potential: purpose, destiny, God's calling and will. **Potential** means unexposed ability, reserved power, undiscovered strength, undiscovered abilities, unused success, dormant gifts, hidden talents and living power. Potential is what we are able to do, but have yet to accomplish; it's the place we can reach, but to which we have yet to arrive. It's who we can become, but have yet to be. It's the ability to imagine that which we have yet to imagine. It is being able to go far, though we have not arrived at that point yet. It is that which we can accomplish, but have yet to do something about. There are many leaders today in this condition; they have yet to develop their potential! If we were to sum this up in a few words, we could conclude that potential is the sum of everything that we are, which has yet to be revealed or manifested. It is a deposit waiting to be loosened and stretched to the limit. We have the ability to be more than we think we can be, more than we can ever imagine, and, do more than we think we can do. This is our potential. Until we try rising to higher levels, to see beyond, or to try something greater, we will never discover our potential.

There are two types of potential, the natural and the spiritual. What is the natural potential? It is the potential with which a person is born. At times, this potential is inherited through the bloodline. The Holy Spirit does not give it, yet He uses it. However, it could be developed through daily living. What is spiritual potential? It is the potential received at the moment we are born again, spiritually. The Holy Spirit gives us this potential. It is also known as purpose, grace, talent, ministry, or function. Every human being was created to develop his potential and to fulfill the calling of God on his life.

What is the principle of "potential"?

The meaning of the seed:

"31 Another parable He put forth to them, saying: "The kingdom of heaven is like a mustard seed, which a man took and sowed in his field, 32 which indeed is the least of all the seeds; but when it is grown it is greater than the herbs and becomes a tree, so that the birds of the air come and nest in its branches." Matthew 13.31,32

There is a potential tree in every seed. For example, I have a mango seed, but in reality, what I am holding in my hand is a potential tree within a seed. God created all things (animals, plants, flowers, birds and more) to live and reproduce according to the principal of the seed.

"[12]And the earth brought forth grass, the herb that yields seed according to its kind, and the tree that yields fruit, whose seed is in itself according to its kind. And God saw that it was good." Genesis 1:12

Every living thing created by God, including man, was blessed with potential.

God deposited in us the ability to be much more than we are at this moment. Just like the mustard seed, we possess hidden resources and abilities yet to be exploited. God gives them to us, they are inside, and the only thing missing is the adequate conditions for them to develop.

What process must the seed go through to develop to its potential?

- Birth
- Death
- Growth

To become leaders, all of us must go through the same process to develop our potential. The order of the steps previously mentioned was established by God, the Sower of the seed. Once God gives the seed, the next step is death. The seed must die in order to be born again; then it will begin to grow. There is no growth without death.

The birth of the seed: This is the time when God, by His reproductive power, gives birth to a seed with potential and power to reproduce; It is when God gives birth to us through His power. When we are born again, this potential is ready to be developed, and the key to accomplish this is to know Jesus as Lord and Savior. In other words, we must be born again. If a man does not have a true encounter with Jesus, it becomes impossible for his potential to rise to the surface. Jesus said: "Apart from me, you can do nothing."

Death of the seed: In this stage, we have to deny ourselves, our ego, and die to our past life. God can't do this for us; we must do it for ourselves.

We must make the decision to obey God, regardless of the price and at the cost of being criticized, if necessary; we must do whatever it takes to develop this potential. During this stage of our lives, we must die to our personal ambitions in order to do the will of God.

Jesus said it this way:

"[24]Most assuredly, I say to you, unless a grain of wheat falls into the ground and dies, it remains alone; but if it dies, it produces much grain. [25]He who loves his life will lose it, and he who hates his life in this world will keep it for eternal life. [26]If anyone serves Me, let him follow Me; and where I am, there My servant will be also. If anyone serves Me, him My Father will honor." John 12.24-26

It is necessary for us to eliminate who we are and die as the seed in order to develop the potential within us. Otherwise, the fruit can never come forth. We must crucify our flesh at the cross, daily, to do the will of God. Remember, this principle always works, and the process the seed must take: birth, death and growth, cannot be avoided.

The seed grows: During this third stage of the process God brings mentors, fathers and leaders to help us grow and develop the potential within us. There are always people that believe in us and who can see beyond what other people can see. They can visualize our potential and help us grow into it. In the following biblical passage, we read how Elijah throws his mantle on Elisha. This demonstrates his ability to identify Elisha's potential, something no one had seen before. There are many men and women like Elijah, raised by God and able to identify people's potential.

"[19]So he departed from there, and found Elisha the son of Shaphat, who was plowing with twelve yoke of oxen before him, and he was with the twelfth. Then Elijah passed by him and threw his mantle on him." 1 Kings 19.19

An illustration of David: No one believed David was capable of becoming a warrior or that he was chosen to be the next king of Israel. *"28Now Eliab his oldest brother heard when he spoke to the men; and Eliab's anger was aroused against David, and he said, "Why did you come down here? And with whom have you left those few sheep in the wilderness? I know your pride and the insolence of your heart, for you have come down to see the battle." 1 Samuel 17.28*

- King Saul said to him, "We can't go against that giant."

  "33And Saul said to David, "You are not able to go against this Philistine to fight with him; for you are a youth, and he a man of war from his youth." 1 Samuel 17.33

  His father did not believe or even contemplate the possibility of David becoming a king, and his brothers were angry with him for defying Goliath. Even King Saul said to him:

  "You can't go against that giant."

  David had potential, but nothing about him proved its existence. Because of this, no one believed in him; it needed to come forth. The world, including his family, set limits to his development. There was one, however, who saw beyond what others could; it was Jonathan. He helped David develop the potential hidden inside of him. From David's example, we can conclude the following: Don't allow anyone to set limits for you. Jonathan believed in David and helped him develop his potential. Potential is not always easily recognized, and it demands to be confronted by a giant in order for it to be brought out into the light, just as David was challenged, forcing his potential to flourish.

  When an individual desires to develop the potential within him, God will use a friend, mentor, father, or someone else who can encourage and believe in him, thus guiding him to his destiny.

What is the source of our potential?

- **God**

Some religious groups say that we are the source of our own potential. This is not true, it is a lie of the devil, because "without God we can do nothing" as the Word teaches us.

"[5]I am the vine, you are the branches. He who abides in Me, and I in him, bears much fruit; for without Me you can do nothing." John 15.5

This truth is extraordinarily special because the potential within us comes from our Creator! Let us keep in mind that the Bible refers to Him as the "Omnipotent". **"Omni"** means full of, and **"potent"** means power in reserve, from which comes the word potential. Hence, it is correct to say that God is always full of **power** and that He is able to do **more** than what He has already done. In other words, God is full of potential and power in reserve. Potential is not in man, but in God, and it is He who gives it. For that reason, it is important to keep in mind God's design in the process of creation. God planned what He wanted to create, He decided the type of material or substance He wanted His creation to be made of, He spoke to the substance of things created, and out of that substance came exactly what He had in mind. To better understand this concept, it can be explained in the following manner:

When God created plant life, He spoke to the earth because that was the substance or the material from which God wanted plants to come from.

"[11]Then God said, 'Let the earth bring forth grass, the herb that yields seed, and the fruit tree that yields fruit according to its kind, whose seed is in itself, on the earth'; and it was so." Genesis 1.11

When God created fish, He spoke to the sea because that was the material or the substance from which He wanted to create them. When He created the stars, He spoke to the heavens because that was the substance from which He wanted them to appear. Everything came forth when He spoke to the substance. When God created man, He spoke to Himself. We come from God because He planned for the substance or the material to create the human race to come from His spirit, because that is what He is. Many of us are unable to discover our potential received at the time of creation because we search for it everywhere except in God, the substance of our existence. Our lives lack fulfillment and our potential is wasted because we search in the wrong places for what is needed to develop it. We try to find our potential through our work, projects, or in other things we produce or create. If we could imagine the fullness of God, our potential would not be on hold.

The Word teaches us that we are born of God. The expression "born again" comes from the Greek word *"gennao"* meaning "born from the genes of". It is in the genes that all inherited characteristics are found. Therefore, from God's DNA come all the characteristics that are in our genes, as well as the potential to become all that God wants us to be. The purpose of anything can't be known if we search for it in places other than in the designer or the Creator. Likewise, the ability of the product to fulfill its purpose is designed within the product. We can't develop our potential if we are not connected to the source, or our creator, God.

The ability to fulfill our purpose is inside of us because we are created by God.

How to develop potential:

We should know the source. We must know God, intimately; He is the only one who knows what we are made of and what our potential is. When we speak of potential we are referring to purpose, calling or destiny. God has the design for our lives; He knows what He created us for, and why. The only way to develop this potential is through a close relationship with our Creator. People might ask: "How can this be accomplished?" Through knowing Jesus Christ as Lord and Savior of our lives.

We should know why we were created. Purpose is the original intention for which we were created. If we desire to develop our potential, we must know our purpose, our calling and what God's will is for us. To discover our purpose we must investigate, seek and ask our Creator why He created us.

We should have a mentor. The mentor assumes the responsibility to develop our potential, purpose or calling. The key word is **"development".** We need men or women to be our mentors and to help us develop our potential. This is the way we'll reach our destiny.

"11 And He Himself gave some to be apostles, some prophets, some evangelists, and some pastors and teachers, 12 for the equipping of the saints for the work of ministry, for the edifying of the Body of Christ." Ephesians 4.11,12

The word "perfection" in the Greek language is *"katartismos"*, meaning to prepare, train or equip. God instituted the five ministries to develop our potential. We all need apostles, prophets, teachers, evangelists or pastors that can teach us, equip us and help us develop the purpose for which we were created.

We must be in the right place. When God created man, He put him in the Garden of Eden, the ideal place for man to grow and develop his potential. Likewise, to develop our potential, it is necessary for us to be in the right place where we can be encouraged to accomplish higher levels of maturity, where we are affirmed and our potential recognized, where the leader identifies our calling and opens doors to help develop it.

We must cultivate our potential. It is essential for us to make the decision to grow. Our potential will never surface until we make the commitment in our minds, plans and dreams, and then, place them in action. We should work or cultivate our potential by seeking the right people, with positive attitudes, that can encourage us and help us succeed. We need to take care of and use the gifts God has given us. We must seek an apostle, or a pastor, an evangelist, a teacher, or prophet with the heart of a father that can help us identify our calling or potential. Then we must serve that person and, as we serve him, God will use him to help us develop our potential or fulfill the purpose for which we were created.

Famous people with hidden potential

Thomas Edison. He was described by a teacher as a "rotten" person, infantile, and a slow learner; his own father came very close to convincing him that he was stupid. Today, thanks to his inventions, we enjoy the benefits of the light bulb and electricity.

Albert Einstein. His parents feared he was stupid. He did poorly in high school, to such an extent that his teacher suggested it was better for him to drop out. The teacher said to him: "Einstein, you will never accomplish anything in life." However, as we know, he developed the theory of relativity.

Walt Disney. He tried seeking employment at a newspaper company, but was told he couldn't draw and that it would be best for him to seek work elsewhere.

Abraham Lincoln. He tried nine times to be elected president and failed. He also ran for governor and senator, and although people remarked he was too simple-minded, it did not stop him. The next time he ran for president, he won the election and was re-elected for a second term. Lincoln was one of the most outstanding presidents in the history of the United States.

Reading these testimonies should encourage us to continue fighting to achieve our goals. Regardless of how many times we fail, if we continue striving, we will accomplish our goals. Every human being has potential that needs to be developed, regardless of the family background, race or nationality. There is potential within all of us, waiting to be developed.

CHAPTER II

What Makes a Leader?

CHAPTER II

What Makes a Leader?

We have the ability and potential to grow as leaders because that was God's design when He created us. From the beginning, God's plan was for man to be lord and leader over all creation, but as previously mentioned, many people die before they have the opportunity to develop their potential; this is truly a tragedy. There are many reasons why this happens and one of those reasons is the environment in which a person lives. When we remain in a place where our leadership potential is not encouraged, it becomes harder for us to be effective leaders. For this reason, we must be close to leaders capable of helping us through the learning process.

"26Then God said, 'Let Us make man in Our image, according to Our likeness; let them have dominion over the fish of the sea, over the birds of the air, and over the cattle, over all the earth and over every creeping thing that creeps on the earth'." Genesis 1.26

Leaders can be classified in two categories according to their potential:

The natural born leader: Some people are born leaders. They wake up in the morning with a hundred things to do, but regardless of how busy they are, everything gets accomplished. When they speak, people follow. An example of leadership are my sons Bryan and Ronald. When they speak, other children follow. They have the natural gift of leadership.

The leader that is created or trained: All leaders are not born with the ability to lead; some emerge with potential for leadership thanks to mentors willing to disciple them and help them grow. When this happens, their growth is quick, not only in ability, but also in gifts. Good mentors are capable of perceiving a person's potential, even when that person can't see it himself. Look for a mentor to help you grow and who can train you to become a leader!

The formation of a leader in the making includes a combination of commitment, discipline, and the desire to grow, learn and mature.

What is a leader?

Leader: An individual with the ability to exert influence, to identify gifts and talents in others, one who has the ability to guide others to their destiny God has for them. When we speak of a leader, we can use different verbs to describe him. For example:

A leader is one who:

- **Encourages.** He does this with words of affirmation at the precise time and when his disciples need it the most.
- **Inspires.** The purest form of influencing others is through inspiration. The opposite of inspiration is manipulation. The genuine leader inspires his followers through his influence.
- **Motivates.** He speaks words of faith to do difficult or apparently impossible tasks.
- **Exerts Influence.** People always surround a leader. He directs them by example.
- **Guides.** The leader guides through vision and purpose. He is constantly confessing, seeing and acting upon that vision. Every time we speak to genuine leaders, their vision is transferred to us; he is sure of what he is doing and knows where he is headed.

- **Mobilizes.** The leader has the ability to bring people together and direct them to achieve certain goals.

- **Activates.** The leader conveys to his followers what God gives him, for example; his gifts, anointing, authority and more. He also awakens dormant gifts in people and activates them to serve God and fulfill their destinies.

- **Persuades.** The leader is able to persuade the people to follow the vision. Leaders have passion and drive to accomplish the vision and the ability to transmit it to others.

- **Disciplines and corrects.** Good leaders understand that discipline is one way to achieve maturity.

Leaders have the ability to inspire others to do what they purpose in their hearts to achieve. Regardless of titles, we will never become leaders unless there are people willing to follow us. The greatest goal of a leader is to inspire his disciples to follow after him. If we had to choose one word from those mentioned above, that one word would be **influence**. Many times we are unaware of when, who, or where we have exerted our influence on others. Did you know that the most introverted person is capable of influencing a **thousand people** during his lifetime?

There are many managers, but few leaders.

Below, you will find a list of characteristics that differentiate a manager from a leader.

Manager	Leader
• He is a copy.	• He is original.
• He notices the smallest details.	• He focuses on the global picture.
• He accepts the status quo.	• He defies the status quo.
• He imitates.	• He is creative.
• He lacks initiative.	• He is innovative.

• He uses manipulation to lead.	• He directs by influence and inspiration.
• Others motivate him.	• He is self-motivated.
• He supervises and keeps people around.	• He is innovative and knows how to help people reach their potential.
• He focuses on the system.	• He focuses on people.
• He is traditional.	• He is always willing to grow.
• His attitude changes according to circumstances.	• He has a positive, stable attitude.
• He is afraid to reproduce himself in others.	• He has the heart of a mentor and father.
• He guards his position.	• He trains others to replace him.
• He condemns others.	• He affirms those around him.
• He works independently.	• He works as a team.
• He observes how things are done.	• He works to make things happen.

It is crucial to understand the difference between a manager and a leader. The desire of every person should be to stop being managers and to become good leaders for the Lord. In my daily walk with God, I have found that great institutions around the world, including large businesses, are full of managers, but very few leaders.

What are the greatest responsibilities of a leader?

1. To be a role model.

"[1]The elders who are among you I exhort, I who am a fellow elder and a witness of the sufferings of Christ, and also a partaker of the glory that will be revealed: [2]Shepherd the flock of God which is among you, serving as overseers, not by compulsion, but willingly; not for dishonest gain, but eagerly; [3]nor as being lords over those entrusted to you, but being examples to the flock; [4]and when the Chief Shepherd appears, you will receive the crown of glory that does not fade away." 1 Peter 5.1-4

What is a role model?

A role model resembles the life of Jesus and His character. Jesus is love, peace, joy, patience, humbleness and has a positive attitude. One of the greatest problems in our youth today is the lack of Christian role models. The search for positive role models in the world today is a difficult task. Some turn to sports, television or music, without success. We need to keep in mind that people follow only if we are models of holiness, purity, integrity and if the love of Jesus is in our homes and character.

When the Apostle Paul made reference of himself as a role model, he wrote it the following way:

"1Imitate me, just as I also imitate Christ." I Corinthians 11.1

"16Therefore I urge you, imitate me." I Corinthians 4.16

The Amplified Bible says: *"Pattern after me, follow my example, as I imitate and follow Christ." "Follow my design, my pattern, my blueprint, as I follow Christ."* Today's youth need to see role models, the image of a leader here on earth. We say to people: "Don't set your eyes on a man," but we have to model after Christ, so those who see us will know Him, know what He is and know what He has done in our lives. Every man is responsible up to the fourth generation that comes after him. If we are good role models now, there will be four generations that will follow us in positive ways based on what they see us do during our lifetime.

What is the best way to become a role model?

Jesus Christ is our model by excellence, but the best way to become a role model is to select a person that follows and imitates Christ. Paul said: "I am the role model, the design, the blueprint. I am the example to follow. Imitate me as I follow the perfect role model, Jesus."

What are the most important areas in which we must imitate Jesus in?

- In the home
- In love
- In integrity
- In service
- In compassion for people
- In the words that come out of our mouths
- In submission
- In our relationship with God
- In the fear of the Lord
- In faith
- In vision

2. To be a mentor or a father.

To be a mentor and to assume responsibility for the complete spiritual development of another person is another great responsibility of a leader. In today's society, we are in need of mentors willing to accept the responsibility of helping young people grow in their calling, and who desire to mature and be successful in life.

What is a mentor or a father?

In the Greek language, the term mentor literally means counselor or wise man. In other words, a mentor is a stable person who does what he says, assumes the responsibility of helping others to grow and mature in their calling and who does this continuously. The mentor has several functions or roles:

- Guide
- Encourager
- Source
- Teacher
- Father
- Protector
- Nurturer
- Provider

"[15]For though you might have ten thousand instructors in Christ, yet you do not have many fathers; for in Christ Jesus I have begotten you through the gospel. [16]Therefore I urge you, imitate me." I Corinthians 4.15-16

The key word for this is **growth**. The question now is: "What kind of growth?"

What we are talking about here is a spiritual, mental, emotional and physical growth. The goal of the mentor is to lead his disciples, his family, and the believers to grow in the calling and purpose God has for them. One of the main characteristics of a mentor is that he has the heart of a father. Without it, it's impossible to achieve the functions or roles previously mentioned. There are many disciples and people in our churches, families and even in large corporations today who desire to grow and mature, but have no idea how to go about doing it because they lack a good role model to follow. They're also in need of a mentor willing to approach them and offer the help needed to grow into their potential.

Another definition of a **mentor** is an individual with virtues we desire to have for ourselves, who accomplishes what we are unable to achieve, who goes where we have not, who is more successful than we are and who has greater anointing and wisdom. In a sense, a mentor is another dimension of a pastor. The only difference is that he continually shares his life with another man or woman through the good example of his conduct and moral values. In the church today, we are in need of leaders willing to assume the responsibility of becoming role models and exemplary mentors. We need them to guide, encourage and evaluate us. They need to be our source of information, to provide the tools we need, to teach us biblical principles for all areas of our lives, and above all, we need them to have the heart of a father to discipline, correct, instruct and give us love.

Regardless of where we are, we will always follow in the path of someone else.

In conclusion, we can say that the greatest responsibility of a leader is to be a good role model and mentor. Many times, we look for leaders without success because we can't identify them. Only a leader can recognize another leader. Today, I will take the opportunity to draw you a picture of what a leader looks like; perhaps you will see yourself in one of these. I find many pastors and businessmen complain that there is a shortage of leaders, but we can't identify leaders around us if we ignore what the profile of a leader looks like.

Profile of a leader:

- He is a visionary (he sees the global picture without concentrating on the small details).
- He is bold, daring, intrepid and assertive.
- He is self-disciplined.
- He has the ability to work with people.
- He makes things happen.
- He takes the initiative.
- He has a good attitude, regardless of the situation.
- He has integrity.
- He knows his calling and the purpose of God for his life, and is able to recognize the same in others.
- He is influential over other people. (people follow him, voluntarily.)
- He has the desire and the hunger to continue growing and learning.
- His desire is to reproduce himself in others.
- He has the desire to serve and submit to others.
- He is trusting.
- He has the ability to communicate with those around him. (he makes himself understood.)
- He is willing to confront any situation; he doesn't run away from anything.
- He doesn't accept the status quo (what is already established).

- He exhibits self-control.
- He knows his identity in Christ.
- He has a close relationship with God.
- He is a peacemaker.
- He depends on God for everything.
- He knows how to handle criticism.
- He doesn't depend on anyone's approval to go on in life.
- He is teachable.
- He has the ability to develop strategies for building a ministry or business.
- He is faithful and loyal.
- He is always in control, even when he is under pressure.

If we were unable to identify ourselves as leaders prior to reading the above characteristics, then perhaps now we can recognize if we are leaders or if we still need to mature in some of the areas mentioned above. Leaders are called to influence and inspire others to fulfill their destinies. They also have the responsibility of being role models and mentors worthy to be followed by a generation in need of men and women to follow. This is why it is of extreme importance that we become a model of integrity and maintain a good relationship with God. We must learn to identify those with a strong potential for leadership and help them to be successful by investing our lives in them. Keep in mind that we are the "eagle" leaders of this generation and God in us will do wonders.

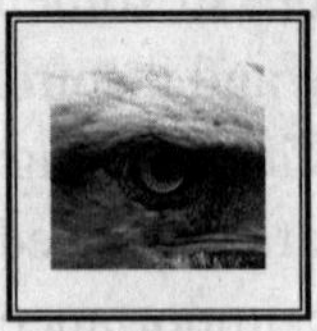

CHAPTER III

Biblical Principles Essential for Leadership

Many books on leadership and its fundamental principles have been written, but what are Jesus' principles of leadership and what are His thoughts on how individuals can become leaders? God's thoughts are not man's thoughts because His ideas concerning leadership are very different from ours. Jesus is the greatest leader that ever lived and, because He is such a leader, we should study His teachings and ideologies concerning leadership and what He said about the essential characteristics a leader should possess. Before going into His teachings, let us take a look at a few important definitions, keeping in mind that there is nothing more powerful than an idea. Creation is the outcome of one of God's ideas and the inventions now in existence are the end product of someone's idea. An idea is a divine seed that can be cultivated to create many things.

What is an idea? It is a conceived, captured or retained thought. It is the mental representation of something or an act of understanding.

What is a thought? It is an unspoken or silent word. This is where ideas and concepts are organized.

What is a word? It is a revealed and exposed thought. The word expresses the idea.

When we speak, we reveal our ideas and expose our way of seeing things. Jesus said, *"From the abundance of the heart, the mouth speaks."* This means that when we speak, who we truly are will be known. All ideas, thoughts and words originally come from God; therefore, if our desire is to have good ideas, then we should go to Him for good thoughts and that way, we will speak His words. When an idea becomes an established thought, then it becomes an ideology.

What is an ideology?

It is an established idea or set of ideas characterizing a person, group, period of time, or a cultural, religious or political movement. For example; three Greek ideologists established democracy. This resulted in many people around the world embracing those established ideas as their own, thus living and leading their lives accordingly. God speaks to us through ideas and thoughts, though oftentimes, we want Him to speak to us through His audible voice. When an ideology is established, then it becomes a philosophy.

What is philosophy? This word can be divided into two parts:

Philo: love

Sophy: understanding, knowing

Therefore, philosophy is the love of knowledge. It is to love what we know and to have intimacy with our thoughts. In modern terms, philosophy means to be in love with our way of thinking or mentality. A philosopher thinks and speaks his own thoughts. We have our own philosophy or way of seeing things that, simply stated, is not a philosophy that comes from God, but from the world. The source of our ideas should be God; otherwise, our philosophy is wrong.

"7For as he thinks in his heart, so is he." Proverbs 23.7

"The way a man thinks in his heart, determines what he is." The word **"heart"** in the Greek language means the subconscious, the place where we store our beliefs. Jesus explains it this way: "The words which I have spoken are spirit and life. If you allow Me to work in you, your mind, your philosophy and your thinking, which you are now in love with, then you will be changed." Jesus declared that what contaminates man is not what goes into the mouth, but what comes out of it.

We think about, become, and have faith in whatever we continually hear. Our faith is limited to what we hear and it comes by hearing the Word of God, continuously.

Then, it is safe to say that the ideas and words we continually hear are very important because they change the way we think. We deal with people according to our philosophy, or our way of seeing things; therefore, it is very important that we understand Jesus' philosophy regarding leadership. Socrates' and Plato's philosophies say there are two types of people: those who are natural born leaders and those who follow. These are examples of incorrect philosophies. When an ideology is established in the mind of people, it becomes their own philosophy or way of thinking. This sets the basis for their beliefs, which in turn, determines their motives and convictions, and eventually directs their actions. In other words, their convictions and motives will be according to their philosophy. The quality of our leadership will only be as good as our philosophy; it is controlled by it. A philosophy that is established for a long period of time becomes a stronghold. This is what the Word of God calls it.

"[4]*For the weapons of our warfare are not carnal but mighty in God for pulling down strongholds."* II Corinthians 10.4

What is a stronghold?

It is an established idea in the mind that predisposes the person to certain ways of reacting. It is a mindset, impregnated with hopelessness, which the individual accepts as fact that a particular situation can't be changed. A stronghold is anything that hinders an individual from doing what God says he can do or becoming what God says he is. Remember the word previously given to us, *"For as he thinks in his heart, so is he."* The end result of certain philosophies is the development of strongholds in our minds, which create a mentality that becomes the basis for every action we take.

A few types of strongholds resulting from false philosophies are:

- Strongholds that set limitations. These are spoken words that cause the mentality of "I can't," "I'm worthless," and "I'm unworthy."
- Deceptive strongholds. When an individual embraces a lie and rejects the truth.
- Philosophical strongholds. These are false doctrines the enemy uses to deceive people.

  "[4]Whose minds the god of this age has blinded, who do not believe, lest the light of the gospel of the glory of Christ, who is the image of God, should shine on them." II Corinthians 4.4

- Strongholds of pride. These strongholds are always looking for ways to exalt the ego, making people think they are better than others.
- Mental strongholds. These thoughts are based on teachings and personal experience that are closed to revelation or God's changes.
- Personal strongholds. These are established patterns of conduct, thoughts and old habits in an individual's mind.
- Strongholds of poverty and despair. These types of strongholds set limitations on people, not only in the personal aspect such as in the home, but the financial area as well.

The reason I have taken time to explain the different types of strongholds is because it is essential for us to erradicate them from our mind. They don't allow us to be or do what God wants, and if our desire is to be effective leaders, we must change our old mentality.

Important aspects we should know regarding thoughts.

- There is someone who always knows what we are thinking, and that person is God.

  "[2]You know my sitting down and my rising up; you understand my thought afar off." Psalms 139.2

- We become what we continually think about.
- Thoughts give way to actions, actions give way to habits, habits give way to character and character gives way to destiny. If we are not careful and neglect to change our way of thinking, our thoughts will make us react accordingly, fulfilling the Scripture that says, *"For as a man thinks in his heart, so is he."*

What are Jesus' fundamental principles on leadership?

1. **Philosophy or way of thinking:** A person reacts and treats others according to the way he thinks. According to Jesus, this is a fundamental principle of leadership, for the way a leader thinks is vital; his success depends on it.

2. **Service or the heart of a servant:** The goal of a Christian leader is his service, not his status. Paul called himself a servant of the Lord Jesus Christ. The Greek word "*doulos*" means servant or slave. A servant is a person who invests his life to serve others, in love.

According to Jesus, these two fundamental principles are needed to become leaders, his philosophy (the way a person thinks) and his service. These assure that the leader has a solid foundation. Jesus established His philosophy or way of thinking to His disciples before doing anything.

"[17]From that time Jesus began to preach and to say, 'Repent, for the kingdom of heaven is at hand'." Matthew 4.17

"Metanoeo" is the Greek word for "**repent**" and it means to change the old mentality, to change the way we think, and to change our mind from what is bad to what is good. Jesus is saying, "Change the way you think; it will make things better. Change wrong thoughts and mental structures brought about by the world, and open up your mind to receive new thoughts that improve your self-esteem, your family and your relationship with God." Jesus also said, "Change your philosophy because the kingdom of God has another philosophy or way of thinking. You are in love with your own ideas or thoughts, but now it is time for change. Your mentality denies the supernatural, it is religious and antiquated. If your desire is to see the kingdom of God manifested with power, it is necessary to change your old mentality. You call yourselves leaders, but manipulate and control the people around you because your philosophy is contaminated. This contaminated philosophy will cause these people not to get along with you." The Lord saw philosophy as the number one priority in His leadership. Before doing anything, He established it. Philosophy creates values. Therefore, if it has a low regard for people, they will be treated according to this low standard. How a leader thinks is crucial because he guides, influences and directs others according to the way he sees things. Because of this, it is important for a disciple to know how his leader thinks. For example, if a person is racist, he will be unable to deal adequately with people.

What is Jesus' biblical philosophy?

Before Jesus spoke to His disciples concerning anything, He established His philosophy through the Sermon at the Mount. In the Beatitudes, Jesus spoke of the philosophy of life in the kingdom of God and how we must change the way we think, our erroneous mentality, and that we must adopt new ways of thinking to help us improve what we do.

I. The Beatitudes

"1And seeing the multitudes, He went up on a mountain, and when He was seated His disciples came to Him. 2Then He opened His mouth

and taught them, saying: "3"Blessed are the poor in spirit, for theirs is the kingdom of heaven. 4Blessed are those who mourn, for they shall be comforted. 5Blessed are the meek, for they shall inherit the earth. 6Blessed are those who hunger and thirst for righteousness, for they shall be filled. 7Blessed are the merciful, for they shall obtain mercy. 8Blessed are the pure in heart, for they shall see God. 9Blessed are the peacemakers, for they shall be called sons of God. 10Blessed are those who are persecuted for righteousness' sake, for theirs is the kingdom of heaven. 11Blessed are you when they revile and persecute you, and say all kinds of evil against you falsely for My sake. 12Rejoice and be exceedingly glad, for great is your reward in heaven, for so they persecuted the prophets who were before you." Matthew 5.1-12

Jesus began teaching and training His disciples on His philosophy beginning with His seminar on the Beatitudes. The beatitudes are nothing more than His mentality, which the disciples received and we should embrace.

"Blessed" is the Greek word *"makarios"* from the root word *"mak"* indicating something that is big or of long duration. It also means blessed, happy to be sent, spiritually prosperous, with life, joy, peace and in God's favor; completely satisfied, regardless of external circumstances. This word can be applied to an individual who is satisfied, not because of favorable circumstances, but rather because he knows how to deal with difficult situations in order to achieve what God has prepared for him. He does so with such joy that it seems as if he were truly enjoying it.

According to Jesus, what should be the mentality of a leader?

Remember, according to Jesus, the two fundamental principles of a leader are his mentality (the way he thinks) and the heart of a servant. Let us take a look at some new ways of thinking, taught by Jesus, in the sermon at the mount.

1. Blessed are the poor in spirit.

"[3]Blessed are the poor in spirit, for theirs is the kingdom of heaven." Matthew 5.3

The phrase *"poor in spirit"* in the Greek language is *"ptocos"*, meaning poor, helpless; a person who regards himself as one needing to be lifted up. Another meaning for the phrase *"poor in spirit"* is an individual who is humble; one who values himself as worthless and insignificant; one who feels small in his own eyes. To be poor in spirit is to lose confidence in one's own justice or strength and to recognize the need for total dependence on God. Jesus is saying, "You will be blessed, happy, envied, spiritually prosperous, with life, joy and satisfied in the favor of God, with salvation. If you are able to understand that you are nothing more than a beggar in your own strength, if you see yourself as insignificant in your own eyes, or in your own strength you are weak and that alone you can do nothing and need someone else to lift you up; that alone you can do nothing and that you need to be humble and recognize your total dependence on God, then your mind will be renewed and you will be prosperous, blessed and totally satisfied.

"[17]Because you say, "I am rich, have become wealthy, and have need of nothing'--and do not know that you are wretched, miserable, poor, blind, and naked-- [18]I counsel you to buy from Me gold refined in the fire, that you may be rich; and white garments, that you may be clothed, that the shame of your nakedness may not be revealed; and anoint your eyes with eye salve, that you may see." Revelation 3.17-18

In this verse, Jesus was not referring to someone lacking material prosperity, rather, He was talking about someone who understood, with deep conviction, that he couldn't do anything in his own strength. Jesus said it best in John 15.5, *"For without Me you can do nothing."* You can't be rich in God until you first become poor in spirit. To be poor in regards to material things means to be without money, or to lack the physical means to sustain oneself, but to be poor in spirit means to be empty inside and to feel a desperate dependency and hunger for God. If our desire is to be rich in God, then we must depend totally on Him. When a man is poor in regards to material things, he has a desperate need for money. When a man is hungry, he has a desperate need for food, but when the spirit of man is poor and empty, he has a desperate need for God. Many believers today, are unaware of whether or not they are poor in spirit. How can we know? Here is a simple example. If you have no money and someone offers you money, you accept it. If you are hungry and someone offers you something to eat, you eat it. If you are experiencing spiritual poverty and someone offers you the riches of God's living Word, the correct reaction on our part would be to accept it. What have you done?

If you are desperate for God, you will always choose Him before your family, a sport, a business or anything else. The poor in spirit choose prayer, the Word and anything else that can get him closer to God. Spiritual poverty is proven when you accept the solution to your desperate desire to know God. As believers, we must choose to change our old mentality and stop choosing other things before God. In conclusion, when Jesus said, *"Blessed are the poor in spirit,"* He meant that if we think we can accomplish great things on our own, then we had better renew our way of thinking and realize that without God we can do nothing. If we are successful in changing our old mentality, we will be truly blessed. The poor in spirit is anyone with a poverty-stricken heart; one who feels he is small, a beggar, or insufficient in his own strength and righteousness; one who is always completely dependent on God for everything. He who is poor in spirit does not set his eyes on the riches of this world, and because he does not set his heart on anything that is temporal, he is content. As the Apostle Paul said, it made no difference to him if he were in lack or living in abundance.

Notice that Jesus said that the most important character trait was humility, dependency on God. Let us not pretend to be great leaders if we are not humble or if we are not totally dependent on God. These qualities are indispensable in a leader's character.

What is the reward of being poor in spirit? You will inherit the kingdom of heaven.

"3Blessed are the poor in spirit, for theirs is the kingdom of heaven." Matthew 5.3

2. Blessed are those who mourn (the afflicted).

"4Blessed are those who mourn, for they shall be comforted." Matthew 5.4

This is another strange blessing. It is not easy to imagine people who are sad being happy, but Jesus say, *"4Blessed (happy) are those who mourn."* What was Jesus referring to when he said, "Blessed are those who mourn?" There is a blessed affliction that qualifies one for happiness, and it includes three types of affliction:

- **Sadness of the guilty party.** This individual cries and feels truly remorseful because of his sin; his genuine repentance leads to salvation. "*10For godly sorrow produces repentance leading to salvation, not to be regretted; but the sorrow of the world produces death.*" *II Corinthians 7.10*. This is sadness felt by a person when he offends God. This sadness is experienced by all born again believers at the moment they accept the Lord and repent of their sins. In other words, Jesus is saying that the second most important truth concerning the character of an individual is to be in the right relationship with God, through the forgiveness of our sins.

- **Sadness experienced by an individual who feels remorseful for the sin of others, love for God and for his neighbor.** These people cry for sinners to know the Lord. This beatitude not only includes feeling remorse for our own sin, but also for the sin of others, as we help them to overcome.

- **Sadness experienced by an individual because of someone else's pain.** These people suffer when they see others going through suffering and affliction, as Jesus cried for Jerusalem. There is so much need in the world, so much pain, hunger and injustice, that Jesus is calling us to change our mentality, to stop being insensitive to the pain of others and to begin crying out for those who suffer, making an effort to help them.

Jesus said, "Those who cry when they offend God with their sin, those who mourn over the sin of others, and those who suffer at seeing the affliction of others are happy, spiritually prosperous, full of life and of peace. They feel satisfied to have found favor in God and are fulfiled." What message is Jesus trying to convey to us? If our mentality or old way of thinking is apathetic to the pain and sins of others, then we must change it. The new kingdom mentality is to mourn for our sins , those who offend God because of their sinful nature and suffer for those who are afflicted. We must learn to be sensitive to the afflictions of others, as well as our own! An illustration of what you have just read occurred when I went to Honduras on a mission trip. I saw children sleeping in the streets, suffering from starvation and nakedness. I was touched so deeply by their suffering that I decided to build an orphanage for homeless children and teach them the Word of God, help them go to school and someday to become successful professional men and women. In the near future, we will be opening other orphanages in Central and South America.

What is the reward of those who mourn? They will be comforted.

"[4]Blessed are those who mourn, for they shall be comforted." Matthew 5.4

3. **Blessed are the meek**.

"[5]Blessed are the meek, for they shall inherit the earth." Matthew 5.5

Meek. This word in the Greek language is *"praotes"*. It describes those that accept God's dealings without resistance or arguments, without murmuring, complaining or struggling against Him. They are provoked, but do not become angry, rather, they remain silent or give a gentle answer. They remain levelheaded while others do crazy things, and they are surprisingly patient and self-controlled while they are stripped of everything they own. They prefer to suffer and forgive twenty insults before seeking revenge for the offense done to them.

Jesus said, "Change your old mentality. If you used to get angry when provoked, if you used to resist God's dealings with you, now I say to you, Be happy, spiritually prosperous, enjoy abundant life, joy and peace." You will experience satisfaction, God's favor and His salvation if you don't resist His dealings with you and if you manage to overcome any provocation without loosing control, but rather remain silent. You will experience God's blessing when you choose to remain silent, to suffer instead of lashing back, and when your patience is strong enough to keep you in control. A meek person becomes angry at the right moment, in the right measure and for the right reason. What is the reward for the meek? He shall inherit the earth. Jesus' message is, "If your attitude is full of complaining and murmuring, if you react in anger when criticized, or when others talk about you, change your mentality and remain silent. Don't return evil for evil. Accept God's dealings in your life without complaint, and change the old mentality for your own good. Then, you will inherit the earth. A genuine leader, according to my philosophy, is an individual who doesn't defend himself when criticized, he doesn't answer back to those who persecute him; he is one who forgives those who offend him.

4. **Blessed are those who hunger and thirst after righteousness.**

"[6]Blessed are those who hunger and thirst for righteousness, for they shall be filled." Matthew 5.6

These people have strong moral and spiritual values in the presence of God. Their desire is to be transparent before Him. They hate sin, are hungry for holiness and have a right relationship with Him. The word "righteousness", according to the Scriptures, is a person that lives in a permanent state of uprightness, integrity and fear of the Lord.

Jesus said: "Happy, blessed to be sent, spiritually prosperous, full of life, joy, peace and fulfilled in God's favor regardless of external circumstances and also in your salvation. Those who have good moral values in My presence, who hunger for righteousness and desire to have a good relationship with Me, they are blessed." We must change our old, corrupt, lying, and hypocritical mentality, for a virtuous and just mentality.

What will be the reward? They will be saturated with God himself. Jesus said, "Get rid of the old mentality because I will not satisfy your hunger and thirst if you continue to live in sin. You must renew your way of thinking. I will fill you as you walk in righteousness and integrity." Jesus teaches us that the pleasures and riches of this life do not satisfy the hunger and thirst within a man's heart; God is the only one who can do that.

5. Blessed are the merciful.

"[7]Blessed are the merciful, for they shall obtain mercy." Matthew 5.7

Merciful: A merciful person will experience anguish when he sees someone else's need or condition. He is merciful, unlike those who simply express an act of mercy because they possess this attribute; he is merciful as a result of God living in him. Those who are merciful do not act this way simply because the need to, but rather, because God inspires them to do so.

Those who comfort the brokenhearted (Job 6.14), those who save others by pulling them out of the fire (Jude 23), and those who feel the pain and suffering of others, will be blessed, happy, spiritually prosperous, experience abundant life, joy, peace, and complete satisfaction. What is the reward for the merciful? *"They shall obtain mercy."* It is also written, "Judgement without mercy will be upon those who are not merciful."

"[13]For judgment is without mercy to the one who has shown no mercy. Mercy triumphs over judgment." James 2.13

What is Jesus' message? His message is that having a teachable heart, a helpful, comforting attitude, and having mercy makes us blessed. His message also states that if we have a tendency to judge people, we must change. The judgmental mentality must be changed into one of mercy and love; otherwise, the day we are in need of mercy, no one will show us mercy, since we have not been merciful towards the fallen.

6. Blessed are the pure in heart.

"[8]Blessed are the pure in heart, for they shall see God." Matthew 5.8

The word *"pure"* in the Greek language is "*katharos"* meaning without mixture, spotless, pure, without contamination, honest, simple, whole, moving in one direction, cleansed through the shakings of life. The idea behind this word "clean" or "pure" is without any dirt; clear water, without mud in it. For this reason, the psalmist would constantly cry out, saying: "*[10]Create in me a clean heart, O God, and renew a steadfast spirit within me." Psalms 51.10.* This is what the character of the believer should be like.

What is the reward? The pure and clean of heart shall see God face to face. Total happiness consists of seeing God, enjoying His favor and having an intimate relationship with Him. Those who are uncontaminated, honest, uncomplicated, and who constantly seek God's pure heart, are "blessed, happy, spiritually prosperous, experience abundant life, joy, peace, and are satisfied to be in God's favor." The person who is pure and clean sees things the way God sees them and sees God in everything. Jesus' message is to exchange the hypocritical, ill-intentioned mind for a pure, clean one. the individual will be the same in private as in public; upright in all areas of his life. In essence, Jesus is saying that to be successful leaders the old mentality must be changed. Wrong motives and intentions must be discarded, and a new mentality full of pure, uncontaminated motives and intentions must replace it. This is the only way to see God in action in our lives.

7. **Blessed are the peacemakers.**

"*[9]Blessed are the peacemakers, for they shall be called sons of God." Matthew 5.9*

Peacemaker is the Greek word *"eirenopoios,"* meaning one who makes peace with others, after first having received the peace of God in his heart. He is not just one who makes peace possible between two parties. A peacemaker is one who ends disagreements. Jesus said, "My philosophy is that peace is better than war. Make every effort to preserve the peace so it will not crumble, and make every effort to repair or fix that which has been broken." Promoting peace is a task that is rarely appreciated and those who dare to settle a disagreement or fight end up hurt themselves by both parties. Understanding this, we should change our mentality and be willing to dissolve ill feelings and cooperate with Christ to bring peace on earth. Jesus is saying, "Change your strife-filled mentality to a pacifist's mentality."

Most people have a hard time promoting peace because they themselves do not have peace with God. A strife filled attitude is a sign that a person lacks the peace of God in his heart.

Jesus is saying we need to change our philosophy concerning peace. Those who seek peace with others are blessed, happy and prosperous. What is the reward of the peacemaker? *"They shall be called sons of God."* Those who are called the sons of God enjoy His peace. Many world leaders are trying to bring peace to their countries and families, but they themselves do not have peace with God because their sins have not been forgiven. Therefore, Jesus said that if you want to be a peacemaker, you should have peace with God first.

8. **Blessed are those who are persecuted.**

"10Blessed are those who are persecuted for righteousness' sake." Matthew 5.10

What is Jesus' philosophy concerning those who are persecuted? This is the greatest paradox of all time and it is exclusive to Christianity. The world thinks happy people are those who are having fun and they admire them. But Jesus regards as blessed those who are persecuted for His name's sake.

How are they being persecuted? *"...They revile and persecute you, and say all kinds of evil against you falsely for My sake." Matthew 5.11*

What will you do when faced with this situation? "*Rejoice and be exceedingly glad, for great is your reward in heaven, for so they persecuted the prophets who were before you." Luke 6.23*

Jesus taught His disciples that persecution was part of **spiritual success.** We will experience persecution at the work place, in school, in politics, in business, in the church and in the family, simply because we think differently than others do; but Jesus said, "Change your mentality." The moment you begin to do anything different in your life, people will criticize you, so stop trying to please people all the time, rather, we should live to please God.

Jesus declared that His philosophy concerning persecution is that persecution is a blessing. Remember, there is one thing human beings can't stand, and that is to watch others succeed. When God prospers us spiritually, intellectually, materially, or in any other form, many will not be able to tolerate it. Therefore, the new mentality that must be adopted is that criticism, persecution and reproach are part of the life of a man or woman who desires to live successfully.

"4Again, I saw that for all toil and every skillful work a man is envied by his neighbor. This also is vanity and grasping for the wind." Ecclesiastes 4.4

What is the reward of those who are persecuted? "*10Blessed are those who are persecuted for righteousness' sake, for theirs is the kingdom of heaven." Matthew 5.10*

Jesus declared that those who are persecuted for His name's sake are happy, spiritually prosperous, enjoy abundant life, have joy and are satisfied to be in God's grace. If, according to Jesus, the number one priority in leadership is to change the way one thinks, or one's philosophy, then let us take a closer look at how to change it.

How can we change the way we think?

"[2]And do not be conformed to this world, but be transformed by the renewing of your mind, that you may prove what is that good and acceptable and perfect will of God. [3]For I say, through the grace given to me, to everyone who is among you, not to think of himself more highly than he ought to think, but to think soberly, as God has dealt to each one a measure of faith." *Romans 12.2-3*

Let us take a closer look at certain key words in this verse from the book of Romans.

- **"Do not be conformed"** – This is the Greek word *"suschimatizo"*, meaning conforming self, in mind and character, to other patterns of thought, or schemes.

- **"Transformed"** – This comes from the Greek word *"metamorpho"*, meaning to change in form. This word refers to a continuous state of change.

- **"Renewed"** – This is the Greek word "*anakainosis"*, meaning to change in order to improve or to rise to a higher level. To exchange the old for the new.

  Re = repeatedly **Newed** = new

  In other words, to put in something new, repeatedly.

- **"Prove"** – This is the Greek word *"dokimazo"*, meaning to rehearse, to test, expecting to approve, to verify that something is worthy.

  If we seal together the meaning of these words, we could say the folowing:

Do not conform in mind or character to the molds and patterns that predominate in the world. Rise to the next level, remaining in a constant state of change through the adoption of new thought patterns, that will improve you so that you may be able to discern, test, and approve the existence of other levels of the will of God that they are worthwhile, good and pleasant.

Then, these are the conclusions that can be drawn from these verses:

- There cannot be any lasting changes in our lives unless there is a **transformation** and a renewing of our mind.
- We cannot rise to other levels of the will of God unless there is a **renewing** of our mind.

What did Jesus say concerning this?

"15...The time is fulfilled, and the kingdom of God is at hand. Repent, and believe in the gospel." Mark 1.15

The word "repent" means to change the way one thinks, a change of mentality, direction and heart.

"22That you put off, concerning your former conduct, the old man which grows corrupt according to the deceitful lusts, 23and be renewed in the spirit of your mind, 24and that you put on the new man which was created according to God, in true righteousness and holiness." Ephesians 4.22-24

What is, then, the process of renovation?

- **Renounce to the old way of thinking.**

  Science has proven that a habit cannot be eliminated, rather, it must be substituted with something else. In other words, we must

substitute the old way of thinking with new thoughts.
How can we do this?

- **Receive the Word.**

  "[21]Therefore lay aside all filthiness and overflow of wickedness, and receive with meekness the implanted word, which is able to save your souls. " James 1.21

- **Meditate on these things.**

  "[8]Finally, brethren, whatever things are true, whatever things are noble, whatever things are just, whatever things are pure, whatever things are lovely, whatever things are of good report, if there is any virtue and if there is anything praiseworthy--meditate on these things." Philippians 4.8

The renewing of your soul results in a new life in Christ. The renewing of our mind is a very important step to maintaining our healing and deliverance. Many people loose what God has given them because they do not renew their minds. Our job as ministers of the Word is to provide the daily word to help you get rid of the old mentality and substitute it for a new one.

According to Jesus, the other biblical principle to be an effective leader is to have:

II. The Heart of a Servant

After Jesus defines His philosophy regarding the principles of leadership, He goes on to teach the other biblical principle for the leader, that is, service. In essence, He is teaching us that the two essential ingredients needed for the making of a leader are his philosophy or way of thinking and the heart of a servant.

"[35]Then James and John, the sons of Zebedee, came to Him, saying, "Teacher, we want You to do for us whatever we ask." [36]And He said to them, "What do you want Me to do for you?" [37]They said to Him, "Grant us that we may sit, one on Your right hand and the other on Your left, in Your glory." [38]But Jesus said to them, "You do not know what you ask. Are you able to drink the cup that I drink, and be baptized with the baptism that I am baptized with?" [39]They said to Him, "We are able." So Jesus said to them, "You will indeed drink the cup that I drink, and with the baptism I am baptized with you will be baptized; [40]but to sit on My right hand and on My left is not Mine to give, but it is for those for whom it is ***prepared."*** *[41]And when the ten heard it, they began to be greatly displeased with James and John. [42]But Jesus called them to Himself and said to them, "You know that those who are considered rulers over the Gentiles lord it over them, and their great ones exercise authority over them. [43]Yet it shall not be so among you; but whoever desires to become* ***great*** *among you shall be your* ***servant****. [44]And whoever of you desires to be* ***first*** *shall be* ***slave of all****. [45]For even the Son of Man did not come to be served, but to serve, and to give His life a ransom for many."*
Mark 10.35-45

Verse 40 states, *"But it is for those for whom it is prepared."* The word "**prepared**" means to be ordained. The Lord said, "Leadership positions are prepared and ordained by my Father." Even when the whole world stands in opposition, God has already established whom He will promote to leadership positions. He determines who will be promoted and in which positions of leadership they will be. Jesus said, "My biblical philosophy concerning how to be a leader is through service." Therefore, He relates greatness with service. Later on, Jesus explained how the world governments lead: ***"They lord over them."*** In other words, they manipulate and control in order to guide and direct people.

Peter puts it this way:

"[2]Shepherd the flock of God which is among you, serving as overseers, not by compulsion, but willingly, not for dishonest gain, but eagerly; [3]nor

as being lords over those entrusted to you, but being examples to the flock." I Peter 5. 2-3

Jesus continues speaking and says, (v. 43) "[43]***Yet it shall not be so among you.***" You must change the way you think; not by force, manipulation, control or beatings, for this is the way the world does things. You must become powerful leaders through serving your own people. Jesus said, **"W*hoever desires to become great among you.*"** The word "great" means if you are going to direct, guide, or become a leader, then you must be a servant. The word **"servant"** comes from the Greek language *"diakono"* meaning minister, servant, slave; one that is always willing to supply the needs of others. Jesus goes on to say, "W*hoever desires to become great among you shall be your servant.*" This refers to one who is higher in rank, first in line, first in order of authority, first in position. The word **"servant"** is the Greek word *"doulos,"* meaning a slave who voluntarily enters into service for the people. He is an individual who is bound to the people at all times. In conclusion, Jesus says, "You have to change the way you think regarding the way a person becomes a leader." Desiring to become a leader is right and good, but to be an effective leader, we need to first serve others. We must become permanent slaves of the people, supplying all their needs.

"[1]This is a faithful saying: If a man desires the position of a bishop, he desires a good work. " I Timothy 3.1

Jesus confirms that it is proper to desire to be leaders. However, the way to become a leader is through becoming a *"diakono"* first, a servant who ministers to the needs of others, and through becoming a *"doulos"*, a voluntary servant, bound to the people at all times, who rejoices as he serves them. Most people around the world lack faith in politicians or governmental figures, because their main interest is in achieving high governmental positions, not in serving the people. Jesus says, "Change your old mentality." If you desire to be remembered as someone great in your nation, organization, church, or anywhere else, then your attitude must be one of service to the people.

You cannot become a leader unless you develop the heart of a servant.

What are the reasons for serving?

- To express gratitude for what Jesus did for us. When you serve, you are saying to the Lord, "Thank you for everything You have done for me."
- To support the growth of the church or organization. God's plan is for every believer to support and serve the local church with His finances, talents, gifts and abilities.
- To make a difference that will last for eternity. When you do what you are passionate about, it will always make a difference in the people around you, and the results will be eternal. If you desire to be an effective leader, then you must make a difference wherever you are by serving the people wholeheartedly, leaving your personal ambitions behind. Exalting God in everything and for everything.

What are incorrect reasons for serving?

- Guilt: This should never be the factor that motivates us to serve the Lord. We should serve out of a thankful heart. When we serve out of guilt, it is nothing more than trying to erase the wrong we have done with good works, but we know that only the blood of Jesus can remove sin.
- Due to pressure: This happens when we tell people there is no one else available to do the job. It is not biblical to pressure people into service. Pressure steals joy; we must serve God with a joyful heart.
- In order to please someone else: This type of service is done when our desire is to please man and not God.

- Pride: Sometimes our desire is to be seen, mentioned and recognized. Thus, we are not serving the Lord but feeding our own ego.

Throughout this chapter, we have reviewed the two basic biblical principles necessary to become leaders. If these principles are not present, none of the others will work. **Our philosophy or way of thinking** determines our way of directing, leading, and how we deal with people. It also determines our actions and values. For this reason, Jesus said it was important to change the way we think. Also, we must develop the **heart of a servant**. As we do this, we will become great leaders making an impact on the world, for the glory of God.

CHAPTER IV

Essential Qualities of a Leader

There are many qualities we can mention that are requirements in the development of leadership, but there are a few essential ones that should be part of the leader's character. A person must have these qualities if he desires to be successful leader. When ministers look within their congregations for leaders to have under their authority, sometimes, they complain because they can't find any around, but in reality, they are around, they just don't know how to identify them. This is why, in this chapter, we will study the profile or essential qualities of a leader.

Essential qualities of a leader:

1. Discipline

Without this quality, the other virtues remain undeveloped. This is the reason why I have listed discipline first in order of priority. Every leader must understand that, prior to conquering the world, he must conquer himself. **What is discipline?** It is the Greek word *"enkrateia,"* meaning to exercise self-control, abstinence from excesses, and self-control in the sense of being steadfast. In other words, it is having a balanced life in every aspect of daily living without falling into extremes. Man's nature is to always live to extremes, either he is radical in his behavior, or he is too permissive because of his sin. God's will is for us to live a balanced life. When we describe a disciplined leader, we say that he is one who is not controlled by his fleshly desires or passions. He is one who exercises self-control and is not a slave to vices or wrong conduct. The disciplined leader is someone who is not given to gluttony, drinking, excessive sleeping, or sexual desires, to mention just a few. In other words, he is someone who knows how to control and dominate all areas of his life.

"[25]And everyone who competes for the prize is temperate in all things. Now they do it to obtain a perishable crown, but we for an imperishable crown." I Corinthians 9.25

A synonym for the word discipline is "self-control"; it is to have control of oneself in every area. I personally believe the success of a leader depends on two things:

Have one's priorities in order.

Have the discipline to carry out these priorities.

Discipline is having control over the mental, emotional and physical areas of our lives, persevering in everything we do and abstaining from the things that tempt us to sin and become distracted from God's purpose for our lives. To be disciplined means to be obedient to our priorities, to be strict and to self-impose certain rules upon ourselves. The most difficult thing for mankind to accomplish is to be self-disciplined.

A personal illustration of self-discipline in my life was establishing the habit of daily prayer. It was difficult at first. My body didn't want to pray every day, nor did I have any emotional desire to do it. But after a while, I recognized that prayer and communion with God was not a religious act, but a priority in my life. Once I understood that prayer was the way to communicate with God, I self-imposed a strict discipline and made a quality decision, a commitment with God, of never leaving home without first talking to Him. This took time, but today, I have better use of my time, and I'm able to achieve more through prayer than I did when I tried to do things on my own.

It is important to recognize who God is. He is the one who gives us the wisdom to make the right decisions in our business, company, ministry or church. I am the pastor of a church with thousands of people, including affiliated churches, and without prayer, it would be impossible for me to do everything that is required of me to do. If it were not for the fact that I have put all my priorities in order and have disciplined myself continually to fulfill them, I would not be as successful in all aspects of my life as I am now.

In I Corinthians 9.25, Paul declares the importance of moderation in all things, meaning that anything in excess is an obstacle in our life that prevents us from advancing.

"[1]Therefore we also, since we are surrounded by so great a cloud of witnesses, let us lay aside every weight, and the sin which so easily ensnares us, and let us run with endurance the race that is set before us. " Hebrews 12.1

Anything in excess in our lives becomes burdens, hindering us from freely running the race. Excess of food, sex, love of money, sleeping, drinking, and so many others, will turn into burdens when you don't have them under control. Therefore, it is very important that we develop a healthy balance in all areas of our life through discipline and with the help of the Holy Spirit.

"[27]But I discipline my body and bring it into subjection, lest, when I have preached to others, I myself should become disqualified." 1 Corinthians 9.27

The Greek word *"hypopiazo"* means to beat the face until it is swollen. This is another way of saying, "I submit my body to permanent slavery." The Amplified Bible says, "*but like a boxer, I buffet my body - handle it roughly, discipline it by hardships - and subdue it.*" and control it daily. I discipline it with difficulty". Every leader needs to be disciplined in all areas of his life, in the home, in his priorities, in his body, in his service to God, in everything. We cannot afford to waste our time in those areas of our lives that slow us down and hinder us from becoming genuine leaders.

A disciplined leader works while others waste their time. He studies while others sleep. He is in prayer while others enjoy themselves and he remains awake into the late hours of the night while others allow sleep to overtake them. The disciplined leader is not lazy. He is different from other people in thought, action, and in the way he dresses and eats. The disciplined leader exercises self-control.

Excess becomes burdensome, causing an imbalance in our life. Discipline is the result of sacrifice, self-denial, surrender and effort. It is the result of a strict and rigorous self-imposed obedience in all areas of life.

2. Purpose

Purpose is the fundamental key to becoming a leader. If we ignore the purpose of God for our lives, then we will be people without direction, motivation or passion. Therefore, it is imperative to know and understand the purpose of God for our lives, so we can fulfill it. When we speak of purpose, we are referring to God's calling and destiny for an individual, his passion, and the will of God for his life.

What is purpose? It is the original intention for which something was created. Everything God created was done with the original intention that it would fulfill its purpose. All created things have a purpose, and that includes you! God created you with a purpose in mind. Often, in Christian circles, we find people asking the following questions: "What is my purpose in life?" "What is my calling?" "What is the will of God for my life?" "What is my passion?" These questions identify people that are still followers and not leaders. A leader knows what God's will is for his life, the purpose for which he was created, what his destiny is, and he understands his calling and his passion. God invites us to fulfill this holy call. It is up to us to discoverGod's purpose and to make the decision to carry it out.

Does everybody have a purpose? Yes, God gave each of us a purpose.

"4Then the word of the LORD came to me, saying: 5Before I formed you in the womb I knew you; before you were born I sanctified you; I ordained you a prophet to the nations. 6Then said I: Ah, Lord GOD! Behold, I cannot speak, for I am a youth. 7But the LORD said to me: "Do not say, I am a youth,' for you shall go to all to whom I send you, and whatever I command you, you shall speak. 8Do not be afraid of their faces, for I am with you to deliver you," says the LORD. 9Then the LORD put forth His hand and touched my mouth, and the LORD said to me: Behold, I have put My words in your mouth. 10See, I have this day set you over the nations and over the kingdoms, to root out and to pull down, to destroy and to throw down, to build and to plant." Jeremiah 1.4-10

Everything God created has purpose; this means that before you were born God had already designed a specific plan for your life.

A leader's real success consists of:

- Knowing the purpose of God for your life.
- Developing this purpose to the fullest.
- Leaving a legacy upon the earth.

As a leader, you cannot guide anyone unless you know the purpose of God for your life. It is impossible to lead someone to a place to which we have not yet been. Discovering the purpose or calling of God for our lives is to find the reason and meaning for our existence. Many people believe that success has to do with having a fortune, being famous or achieving high governmental positions, to have a number of thriving businesses, to have a large church or a recognized ministry. These things are good, but they only represent success according to man's standards and none have anything to do with success according to God's standards. However, if we are interested in being successful according to God's standards, then we need to know the purpose for which we are here on earth, develop it and leave a legacy. Once this is achieved, then we can consider ourselves successful men and women.

The anointing of God is found in His purpose.

"[1] I, therefore, the prisoner of the Lord, beseech you to walk worthy of the calling with which you were called." Ephesians 4.

The word **"calling"** means career or profession. The same way there are doctors, engineers and lawyers, there are also careers in God. What is yours? It is **your** job to find out! You will never be completely happy and satisfied until you understand and fulfill God's purpose in your life.

How can you know if you are carrying out the purpose of God in your life?

Here are some keys that can serve as a guide to discover and understand the purpose for your existence.

- If what you are doing is satisfying, and you feel peace, joy and fulfillment with what you are doing, then you are in your purpose and calling.
- When you make a difference in others. When you are carrying out the purpose of God for your life, His anointing and power back you up and you will make a difference everywhere you go.
- When other people are edified or built up by what you do. God's gift is given to you to edify and minister to others. Because of this, when you minister, people are edified in supernatural ways, thus implying that you are in the right calling.

- When you have great passion for what you are doing. Passion is a vital and distinctive tool used to recognize the purpose of God. The message is, if you don't feel passion for what you are doing, then, that is not your calling. **Passion consists in the willingness to go through, and survive, the process to achieve your dream.**

- Renewing your understanding. One way to understand the will of God for our lives is through the renewing of our minds.

Because leaders know their purpose or calling, they are able to guide others to fulfill their destiny. It is important to seek and to embrace the will of God for our lives to be effective in leadership.

3. Integrity

"7In all things showing yourself to be a pattern of good works; in doctrine showing integrity, reverence, incorruptibility." Titus 2.7

The foundation of the character of every believer and of a leader is integrity. You cannot follow someone who does not walk in integrity, because one of the things that this walk creates is **credibility**.

What is integrity? It is the ability to be the same in public as well as in private. An individual with integrity is not double-minded, and remains in control regardless of external pressures. A person with integrity says, "I am who I am regardless of where I am, what circumstances surround me, or who I am with. I am the same when I speak and when I act."

What qualities are found in a person with integrity? A person of integrity has an irreproachable character, his motives are pure; he is uncorrupted, pure, complete and unified in body, soul and spirit. Men and women of integrity do what they say they are going to do, even when no one is watching them. A leader with integrity is not deceitful, but loyal; he is not double-minded or a hypocrite. He is everything he appears to be and his mind is undivided. The leader who lives in integrity has nothing to hide, nothing to fear; and his life is an open book.

"[9]He who walks with integrity walks securely, but he who perverts his ways will become known." Proverbs 10.9

To detect your level of integrity, ask yourself the following questions:

- Am I on time for my appointments?
- Do I keep my promises?
- Am I the same in public as I am in private?
- When something is done, do I give credit where it is due, or do I take credit for myself?
- Do I lie when I am under pressure?
- Do I treat my family the same at home as I do at church or at home?
- Do I give free reign to bad thoughts?

Integrity is a character trait of a true leader; it builds confidence, and it is essential in a leader for others to follow him.

4. Vision

"[6]My people are destroyed for lack of knowledge. because you have rejected knowledge, I also will reject you from being priest for Me; Because you have forgotten the law of your God, I also will forget your children." Hosea 4.6

"[18]Where there is no revelation, the people cast off restraint; but happy is he who keeps the law." Proverbs 29.18

One more essential quality of a leader is that he is a visionary. People with vision impact the world in one way or another; this is the first step to becoming a successful leader. Vision brings order to the reaching of goals and purpose of the organization. We should also build our family with vision, without it, we take the risk of wasting resources and living without limits or direction. Helen Keller was asked, "Is there anything worse than being born blind?" Her answer was, "To have eyesight without vision." The worst leader is not one who lacks material goods, but one who lacks vision. Successful leaders are motivated by something greater than themselves; a dream seemingly beyond their reach, yet they remain convinced that they have the ability to attain it.

What is vision? It is the revelation of God's plan, and purpose for a man or woman. Vision should be born out of an intimate relationship with God. Many visions are simply personal plans and ambitions of individuals, who have not had an intimate experience with God.

The vision that isn't born in an intimacy with God becomes the source of division. In other words, for it to be God's vision, we must ask Him what He wants and receive it during our time of intimacy with Him.

In other words, when everyone has the same vision, it is because it was born out of God's heart. However, when everyone has a different vision, or different versions of it, the result is division.

There are three Hebrew and Greek words used to describe the word vision. These words have interesting meanings:

- **Chazon:** A word from God received in intimacy.
- **Optasia:** Derived from the word optical, meaning to see beyond, to see a little bit of our future.
- **Jorasis:** The ability to perceive or discern, with eyes of faith, the dream God places in one's heart.

To whom does God give a vision?

God gives vision to a man or woman, never to a council, organization, or committee. God always gives the vision to a man, such as happened with Moses, Jeremiah and others.

To whom does the leader transmit the vision?

To leadership

Once a man or woman of God receives God's vision, then the leadership is in charge of transmitting it to the people, as in the case of Moses, when he passed the vision down to the seventy elders.

"[17]Then I will come down and talk with you there. I will take of the Spirit that is upon you and will put the same upon them; and they shall bear the burden of the people with you, that you may not bear it yourself alone." Numbers 11.17

To the people

The people, together with the leadership, are in charge of taking the vision that God gave a man or woman and making it a reality. Leadership and the people are given by God to help carry the burden and develop the vision.

How can you help carry the burden for the vision God has given your leader?

- Understanding the vision: This consists of having a clear concept of what the vision is, and surviving the process regardless of the price.

- Taking hold of the vision: This means appropriating the vision of the local church, and making a commitment to it.

- Contributing to the vision: With financial support, service, prayer, talents and abilities.
- Passing the vision on to others; multiplying oneself in others, talking to them about the vision.

The success of a leader is not measured by how many people understand the vision, but by how many take hold of the vision, making it their own, and contribute to developing and sharing it.

What does the vision give to the leader?

Vision gives the leader passion and desire to survive the process. It personally motivates him during difficult times, giving the people direction to follow him as it strengthens him to go ahead.

What strategies are needed to carry out the vision?

"1Now the whole earth had one language and one speech. 2And it came to pass, as they journeyed from the east, that they found a plain in the land of Shinar, and they dwelt there. 3Then they said to one another, "Come, let us make bricks and bake them thoroughly." They had brick for stone, and they had asphalt for mortar. 4And they said, "Come, let us build ourselves a city, and a tower whose top is in the heavens; let us make a name for ourselves, lest we be scattered abroad over the face of the whole earth." 5But the LORD came down to see the city and the tower which the sons of men had built. 6And the LORD said, "Indeed the people are one and they all have one language, and this is what they begin to do; now nothing that they propose to do will be withheld from them."Genesis 11.1-6

The building of the Tower of Babel is a biblical example of how to carry out the vision. Although the men building the tower were not doing God's will, they were applying biblical principles in order to reach their goal. Let us take a look at these principles:

- **Unity** – Every time a leader and the people unite, there will be a multiplication of power and anointing. To see God's vision become a reality, there must be unity and when this happens, there will be a multiplication of power.

- **Communication** – Speaking the same "language," and comunicating it to the leadership and the people. Leaders must inspire the people to speak the same language, thus bringing everyone together in one spirit.

- **Commitment** – Making the decision to wholeheartedly remain in the vision, not only for a brief period of time but for the long haul as well, with no turning back, until what was purposed is carried out.

- **Perseverance** – "There is nothing that can make us turn back." To do something until completion requires commitment and unity, and as a result, a multiplication of power. When the same language and vision is shared, the planned objectives can be accomplished.

5. Dealing with people

This is another very important characteristic of a leader. A survey was taken among a number of large corporations in order to determine the reason why customers were not coming back. The results were as follows:

1%	Clients die.
3%	Clients move away.
5%	Clients have friends in other companies.
9%	Competition.
14%	Clients are dissatisfied with the product.
68%	An attitude of indifference towards the clients. Poor customer service.

The result of this survey helps us understand that our success or failure is determined by how we treat people. People will not follow a leader who continuously mistreats them. People are looking for leaders to speak words of encouragement and praise to them, to help them, love them, to be interested in them, and to discipline them when necessary.

How should we treat people?

12Therefore, whatever you want men to do to you, do also to them, for this is the Law and the Prophets." Matthew 7.12

Once again, as was previously mentioned, we will treat those around us according to our philosophy or way of thinking.

What is the biblical philosophy regarding how one should treat people?

- **People are more important than anything else is:** they are more important than a building, a system, a method, or an organization.

  *"30Then Jesus answered and said: "A certain man went down from Jerusalem to Jericho, and fell among thieves, who stripped him of his clothing, wounded him, and departed, leaving him half dead.
  31Now by chance a certain priest came down that road. And when he saw him, he passed by on the other side. 32Likewise a Levite, when he arrived at the place, came and looked, and passed by on the other side. 33But a certain Samaritan, as he journeyed, came where he was. And when he saw him, he had compassion. 34So he went to him and bandaged his wounds, pouring on oil and wine; and he set him on his own animal, brought him to an inn, and took care of him. 35On the next day, when he departed he took out two denarii, gave them to the innkeeper, and said to him, "Take care of him; and whatever more you spend, when I come again, I will repay you.' 36So which of these three do you think was neighbor to*

him who fell among the thieves?" [37]And he said, "He who showed mercy on him." Then Jesus said to him, "Go and do likewise."Luke 10. 30-37

- **Every human being is our neighbor:** The Word of God teaches us that every human being is our neighbor, and that we must love them because it is a commandment of God, regardless of color, race, social status, intellectual level or nationality.

[43] "You have heard that it was said, "You shall love your neighbor and hate your enemy.' [44]But I say to you, love your enemies, bless those who curse you, do good to those who hate you, and pray for those who spitefully use you and persecute you". Matthew 5.43,44

"[2]Let each of us please his neighbor for his good, leading to edification." Romans 15.2

The principle of sowing and reaping:

"[7]Do not be deceived, God is not mocked; for whatever a man sows, that he will also reap..." Galatians 6.7

If we, as leaders, could understand this basic principle, it would be the beginning of great changes in our lives. If we treat others badly, we will be treated the same way. If we sow love in people, then we will receive love; but if we sow mistreatment, that is what we will receive. If we give of our time to listen to others, we will receive the same. To be able to understand people, we must know the basic needs of every human being:

- **Love** – Every human being has a deep-seated need to be loved, and where he receives love, he will contentedly remain.

- **Respect** – One thing that keeps human relationships healthy is respect. When we receive this respect, then we feel valuable as human beings.

- **To be listened to** – Listening is an art not all people have developed, even when there is a dire need for it. Most people know how to hear, but few have learned to listen.

- **Affirmation** – People are anxious to hear a word of affirmation, encouragement, and appreciation concerning their identity, their job, their calling and their person. People desire to hear a word of praise or a word of approval to raise their low self-esteem. They need to hear someone say, "I believe in you: I trust you."

Let us see how Jesus treated people.

"[35]Then Jesus went about all the cities and villages, teaching in their synagogues, preaching the gospel of the kingdom, and healing every sickness and every disease among the people [36]But when He saw the multitudes, He was moved with compassion for them, because they were weary and scattered, like sheep having no shepherd." Matthew 9.35,36

Jesus treated people with compassion; it was the key to all of his miracles. Taking into consideration what was written in previous chapters, we can say that compassion is the key that enables us, as leaders, to treat people well. If compassion for people is our main motivation, then we will be able to love, respect, listen to, and affirm them. Jesus knew that compassion for God and for the people, was essential to being an effective leader; that is to say, a vertical and horizontal relationshipp.

Following are a few questions we should ask ourselves to know if we push people away from us or attract them closer to us:

Are you a person who pays too much attention to the race or to the intellectual level of others? Do you make effective decisions or do you feel insecure when you make them? Are you afraid someone is going to take over your position? Do you feel envy or jealousy when other people succeed? Are you moody? Do you consider yourself to be a perfectionist? Can you handle criticism or do you feel depressed when criticized? Do you have a positive attitude towards life? Do you follow through on what you say you are going to do?

How should you deal with difficult people?

Difficult people with different personalities can be found everywhere we go. The question is how to deal with them. How should we treat them? Difficult people are found at the workplace, in the church, at home, in sports. They are everywhere. Therefore, as leaders, it is important to learn how to deal with them.

What should be the basic biblical principle when dealing with difficult people?

"[19]Therefore thus says the LORD: "If you return, then I will bring you back; you shall stand before Me; If you take out the precious from the vile, you shall be as My mouth. Let them return to you, but you must not return to them." Jeremiah 15.19

If we want to be effective leaders, we cannot allow these people to influence us. We cannot compromise our principles, surrendering to their whims and wishes. We must use God's wisdom to restore and help them without behaving as they do.

What type of difficult people must we deal with on a daily basis?

Manipulators – These people want to manipulate and control circumstances and their surroundings. They step on anyone in order to remain in control. Let us take a closer look at this type of behavior.

What is the root of manipulation and control?

- **Insecurity** – These people are insecure about who they are. They don't know who they are or what they have. As a result, they always need to be in control because this is the only thing that gives them the illusion of security.

- **The Jezebel spirit** – Sometimes, these people may be under the influence of the Jezebel spirit, which manipulates and controls.

  "[20]Nevertheless I have a few things against you, because you allow that woman Jezebel, who calls herself a prophetess, to teach and seduce My servants to commit sexual immorality and eat things sacrificed to idols. *Revelation 2.20*

How should you deal with a manipulative individual?

- Confront him with his problem. This type of person needs to know why he is behaving this way.

- Offer him help. Confronting this individual with his problem is not enough; a solution needs to be offered to him.

What is the solution?

- Affirm him in his identity. Let him know how precious and unique he is in God's eyes. It is important to teach him that his security is found in Christ, and not in his position.

- Ministering inner healing and deliverance. Generally speaking, the background of those who are controlling and manipulative is that of abuse, suffering and abandonment. These situations make these people act the way they do. Therefore, one way to help them is to minister inner healing and deliverance.

Hot tempered people. This type of individual explodes and becomes extremely angry for little or no reason. He has unpredictable bursts of anger. In His presence, we must walk on egg shells all the time because it is uncertain when his volcanic temper will erupt. This person is unpredictable.

"[32]He who is slow to anger is better than the mighty, and he who rules his spirit than he who takes a city." Proverbs 16.32

"[11]The discretion of a man makes him slow to anger, and his glory is to overlook a transgression." Proverbs 19.11

How should you deal with this type of people?

- Always respond to them with a soft answer.

  "[1]A soft answer turns away wrath, but a harsh word stirs up anger." Proverbs 15.1

  This type of personality cannot be controlled if given an answer in anger; only a soft one will do. If they are responded to angrily, it causes more tension.

- Confronting them with their anger problem. The Word of God teaches us that people who cannot control their anger cannot be good leaders because what has taken years to build can be demolished in a minute as a result of their anger.

Extremely sensitive people. These individuals get their feelings hurt over everything; we must continually give them spiritual massages to keep them going.

How should you deal with extremely sensitive people?

- Confronting them with their problem. For the most part, these people are easily hurt because they have a problem with rejection.

They have roots of rejection, fear of being rejected, and self-rejection. They take everything personally.

- They need emotional healing. As a pastor, I cannot have people like these as leaders because sooner or later, they will hurt others due to their own problems. We cannot discard them as leaders, but we have to work with them in order to heal them.

The "pity party" people. These people pity themselves, and use this attitude to manipulate others. They constantly complain and remember everything that happened to them in the past. They want people to feel sorry for them.

How should you deal with these people?

- Confront them with their negative attitude. We should correct them in a strong, firm manner to awaken them from their "pity party" dream. They cannot be spoken to in a soft manner, because it makes the problem worse.

- They must be held responsible for the environment they are creating. If they remain negative, inevitably, it will contaminate the whole body. They must make a decision to stop complaining and to stop feeling sorry for themselves.

People who are "users." These people use others to accomplish their own objectives and goals. These people manipulate to benefit themselves using all kinds of tactics. They are looking to carry out their own agendas, without giving a second thought to the needs of others.

How should you deal with these people?

- Learn to say "NO". There are times when it is difficult for us to say "NO". Unfortunately, many people wait for the opportunity to take advantage of our kindness; therefore, we must learn to give them a firm "NO" at times.

"[37]But let your "Yes' be "Yes,' and your "No,' "No.' For whatever is more than these is from the evil one." Matthew 5.37

People with low self-esteem. These individuals believe they are worthless.

How should you deal with them?

- Teach them who they are in Christ. God gives every human being potential, a purpose, a calling, and the ability to carry it out.

- Continually affirm them. Every leader must affirm the people God places around him, particularly those with low self-esteem.

Stubborn and rebellious people. These people want to do things like Frank Sinatra, *"I did it my way."* They don't like to submit to anyone and are always questioning their leader's authority.

How should you deal with them?

- Rebellion is demonic. They must be taught that rebellion is the principle used by the enemy to rebel against God.

- Find out the reason for the rebellious attitude: Some people are rebellious because they were abused by those in authority, and as a result, they consider any authority over them to be excessive and out of control.

In conclusion, we can say that if we desire to be effective leaders, we must learn to deal with all types of people, even with those who have difficult personalities.

What can we ask God to help us deal with difficult people effectively?

- **Wisdom.** This consists in finding out the root of all things, visible and invisible.

  Before we correct, admonish or encourage anyone, we must ask ourselves, "What is the root of his problem?" We need to ask God for wisdom to find out the root of the person's behavior.

  "[5]If any of you lacks wisdom, let him ask of God, who gives to all liberally and without reproach, and it will be given to him." James 1.5

- **Agape love.** This type of love is given unconditionally to others, without expecting anything in return. This kind of love believes in people, regardless of their shortcomings. It believes that people are capable of changing someday.

6. A seeker of God

Every good leader understands that everything he has rotates around his total and absolute dependence on God; therefore, an essential quality in a leader is that he be a seeker of the presence of God. Everything we are and everything we have is the result of having daily communion with God. All other virtues are dependent on this • one quality. Therefore, it becomes necessary that we have a strong, profound and consistent devotional life with God.

What does the leader's devotional life with God consist of?

- **Prayer** – Having communion with the Father every day. We are not talking about something sporadic, but rather of something that is done on a daily basis.

- **Read and study the Word** – God speaks to us daily through His Word. It is necessary for us to read it and live it every moment because it will bring changes to our lives.

- **Regularly attending the local church** – Every leader must know the importance of attending a local church and of having a pastoral covering.

"[25]Not forsaking the assembling of ourselves together, as is the manner of some, but exhorting one another, and so much the more as you see the day approaching." Hebrews 10.25

We can be disciplined people, with purpose, vision, and integrity, we might treat people well, but if we don't have an intimate relationship with God, we will be ineffective and none of the other qualities will help. The leader cannot begin his day without spending time talking with the Lord and pouring out his soul in His presence. All wisdom and peace needed to work throughout the day come from God when we seek Him in prayer.

7. Bold and courageous

A few qualities of a good leader are boldness, audacity, and the quickness with which he attacks any adverse situation or circumstance. The opposite of boldness is fear. Courage comes to an individual as the result of his intimate communion with God.

"[32]Those who do wickedly against the covenant he shall corrupt with flattery; but the people who know their God shall be strong, and carry out great exploits". Daniel 11.32

In this verse, the word **"know"** means "to have intimacy with." The word **"carry out"** means to do daring and powerful deeds. If we interpret this correctly, it could be stated in the following manner, "Those who have an intimate relationship with their God, will do bold, powerful things."

What is audacity? This word is translated as **boldness**. In the book of Acts, it is the word *"parrhesia,"* meaning audacity, boldness, and courage to speak and to act.

Audacity and boldness come to a person as a result of his intimate communion with God. They are not innate human qualities.

"[31]And when they had prayed, the place where they were assembled together was shaken; and they were all filled with the Holy Spirit, and they spoke the word of God with boldness." Acts 4.31

Every leader should have the boldness and audacity to believe for great things, to believe in others and to trust God. We must have audacity to cast out demons, the boldness to protect what belongs to us, the courage to testify about Christ, the boldness to begin new business ventures, the audacity to believe for great projects and to face problems head on. Genuine leaders confront the problems in their families, in their companies, ministries and nations. They have the courage to face problems and come up with a solution even at the expense of their own lives.

What is courage? Dr. J. Oswald Sanders defined courage as "the mental ability that allows people to face danger with firmness, fearlessness and without discouragement." History tells us that Martin Luther is regarded as one of the boldest and most courageous men to ever live. When he departed on his journey towards Worms to face the questions and controversies his teachings incited, he said: "You can expect anything from me, except fear or retraction. I will not run, even if demons were as numerous as the tiles on the roof, I will go to Worms." All leaders should be bold, courageous, full of valor and fearless when facing danger. People expect us as leaders to be strong and courageous during times of crisis. While others lose their heads, leaders remain stable when faced with danger. Leaders encourage their followers in the midst of difficult situations and discouragement.

A biblical example of this is the case of Hezekiah.

"[7]Be strong and courageous; do not be afraid nor dismayed before the king of Assyria, nor before all the multitude that is with him; for there are more with us than with him. [8]With him is an arm of flesh; but with us is the LORD our God, to help us and to fight our battles." And the people were strengthened by the words of Hezekiah king of Judah." 2 Chronicles 32.7,8

We can conclude that boldness and courage should be essential qualities of a leader. We need these virtues to attempt great things and to face danger without fear or cowardice in our hearts.

8. **Humility**

"[5]Let this mind be in you which was also in Christ Jesus." Philippians 2.5

Humility is another essential quality of a leader. It is vitally important that a leader understands what it means to be humble.

What is humility? This word comes from the root word "*humus*" meaning soil, from which is derived the word "human". Therefore, we can define humility as the ability to recognize that we are simply human and that everything we are and have comes from God. In other words, there is nothing we can produce by ourselves because we are human beings, and this, only by the grace and favor of God. Another definition for the word **humility** is the ability to transfer glory and recognition. Every leader must understand that what he is and what he has belongs to God. Therefore, he must learn to give God the glory, not only in private, but in public. Often, we hear men say just like Paul: *"[9]For I am the least of the apostles, who am not worthy to be called an apostle, because I persecuted the church of God." I Corinthians 15.9*. Later on in another Scripture, another declaration is made: "*[8]To me, who am less than the least of all the saints, this* *grace was given, that I should preach among the Gentiles the unsearchable riches of Christ." Ephesians 3.8.* John the Baptist used the phrase; *"[30]He must increase, but I must decrease." John 3.30.*

Dr. Brengle described this in his notes: "If I appear great before their eyes, the Lord, in His great kindness, is helping me to see how little I am without Him. He helps me remain small before my own eyes. The Lord uses me effectively, but I want to be sure it is Him who is using me and not my own works. The ax cannot glorify itself for cutting down the trees. It can't do it by itself; it needs the lumberjack. After all, he is the one who made the ax, sharpened it and used it. As soon as he sets it aside, the ax becomes nothing more than old iron. Oh, that I never lose sight of that!"

The humble leader recognizes his weaknesses and his strengths. He does the job others do not want to do and also works behind the scenes; he does not look for recognition.

9. Decisive

When he realizes what the will of God is, a leader makes clear and timely decisions. This is the sign of a true leader. **A visionary can see, but a leader makes wise decisions.** I have met leaders that are inconsistent in their decision-making. They don't know what they want and lack conviction in the area of their values and principles. In other words, they are leaders who stand on the side of the enemy one day and on God's side the next. When Moses decided to leave Egypt he left behind everything that was ficticious and apparent, the false splendor of that great empire, including all the privileges he enjoyed as the son of the Pharaoh's daughter, and he identified himself with the Hebrew slaves. This decision, years later, allowed him to do great things that later identified him as one of the most renowned patriarchs of the Old Testament. Every leader must learn to make decisions at the right time, without expecting to please all the people, all of the time. Decisions must be made at the moment the will of God is known, even though it may not be the most popular decision, or even if it is the most controversial. We must be leaders with the ability to decide and not be indecisive. We must be sure of what we want and where we are going. Nothing should stop us from becoming decisive people except God himself. An example of a man with the ability to make decisions can be observed in our President George Bush. Regardless of the thousands of people protesting the war against Iraq, the criticism of great television stations, and countries such as Germany, France and Russia opposing him, he still made the decision he believed to be the right one. He went to war, delivered a country from the hands of a tyrant who was a threat to humanity, the United States of America and Israel. Finally, the victory was his. God gave him grace and favor, and because of this, there is a nation that now enjoys the freedom made possible by a man who has the ability to make decisions, regardless of the opposition.

10. Faithful and Loyal

It is essential for leaders to be faithful and loyal at the same time. This virtue is part of the leader's character. Therefore, it is important that we understand what it is and how to develop it.

What does it mean to be faithful? It is the ability to do a job consistently, without quitting or fainting. A faithful person can be depended upon to do the specific job assigned to him; he can be trusted.

What does it mean to be loyal? It is the ability not to betray and to be completely committed to an individual.

A faithful person is committed to do the task he has been asked to do. A loyal person is committed to the individual who gave him the job. Many leaders are faithful. They do their job well and consistently, but they are not loyal because they speak against their employer, their pastor, or the person they work for. They join others to criticize and betray the person to whom they are committed. Every leader should learn to be faithful and loyal, all the time.

Biblical Illustration: The case of Amasa was a general in David's army. *"[13]And say to Amasa, 'Are you not my bone and my flesh? God do so to me, and more also, if you are not commander of the army before me continually in place of Joab'." 2 Samuel 19.13.* King David had a son named Absalom, who one day rebelled against his father. As a result of that rebellion and division, one of David's faithful men, named Amasa, abandoned the king.

"[25]And Absalom made Amasa captain of the army instead of Joab. This Amasa was the son of a man whose name was Jithra an Israelite, who had gone in to Abigail the daughter of Nahash, sister of Zeruiah, Joab's mother." 2 Samuel 17.25

Amasa was faithful in his job as general in David's army. He was always on time, did his job consistently, prepared the supplies every day, trained the soldiers faithfully, and never left his job unattended. He was very faithful, but he was not loyal. He demonstrated this when the trumpet of rebellion was heard, and he was the first one to abandon David to become a leader in Absalom's army. After some time, Absalom died and King David called Amasa back. He forgave him for what he had done, restored him and brought him once more into his army.

"[13]And say to Amasa, Are you not my bone and my flesh? God do so to me, and more also, if you are not commander of the army before me continually in place of Joab'." 2 Samuel 19.13

On another occasion, David suffered yet another act of rebellion, but this time Sheba was the culprit.

"[1]And there happened to be there a rebel, whose name was Sheba the son of Bichri, a Benjamite. And he blew a trumpet, and said: "We have no share in David, Nor do we have inheritance in the son of Jesse; Every man to his tents, O Israel!" [2]So every man of Israel deserted David, and followed Sheba the son of Bichri. But the men of

Judah, from the Jordan as far as Jerusalem, remained loyal to their king." 2 Samuel 20.1,2

The King sent Amasa to gather the men, but instead of returning to the King, he remained in Sheba's camp and betrayed David again.

"[4]And the king said to Amasa, "Assemble the men of Judah for me within three days, and be present here yourself. [5]So Amasa went to assemble the men of Judah. But he delayed longer than the set time which David had appointed him." 2 Samuel 20.4,5

In the end, Amasa died covered in blood. What led to his death? His disloyalty to King David was his downfall.

"[12]But Amasa wallowed in his blood in the middle of the highway. And when the man saw that all the people stood still, he moved Amasa from the highway to the field and threw a garment over him, when he saw that everyone who came upon him halted." 2 Samuel 20.12

Get the job done and be committed; not only to the task, but to the person in authority. Don't allow anyone to betray the person that entrusted his heart and life to you. You must be loyal. The essential virtues of an effective leader can be summed up the following way: He has purpose and knows where he is going. He is disciplined, and lives in integrity; that is, he is the same in public as well as in private. He is a visionary. He treats people around him well and with compassion. He seeks God with all his heart. He is bold and humble. He recognizes that everything he has and everything he is comes from God and he is decisive, loyal and faithful.

CHAPTER V

How to Confront Effectively

CHAPTER V

How to Confront Effectively

The word **"confront"** may seem a bit strong, but I personally believe that avoiding a confrontation makes a situation worse. There are many situations that rise within the church, at the workplace, the office, and business; many situations worsen because we are afraid to confront the people with their problems. In this chapter, we will discuss how to confront effectively in order to bless others.

What does it mean to confront?

To confront is to lead someone to the reality of his situation and the realization that change is needed.

Nobody likes to hear the truth. Jesus said the truth in the Word is like a two-edged sword that sometimes cuts through and other times, it heals the wound. It is necessary that each one of us be confronted with the truth of our character, the situations in our home, and many other areas.

What should our intention and purpose be for confronting people?

1. **Love** – When an individual is confronted with a problem, it is because he is loved. The correct expression should be, "I love you so much that I must confront you and tell you the truth." The reason we confront people should be love. If we don't tell them the truth, we become contributors to their downfall. Many people don't believe, or are unaware that they have a problem that needs to be confronted with the truth, but someone who truly loves them needs to do it.

2. **Confront to correct what is wrong** – You cannot correct what is wrong if it is not confronted. If we desire to correct something in our personal life, in the church, at the workplace, or at home, we must

learn to confront. It is not easy to do it at first. There are people who avoid confrontation at any price because they do not want to see themselves involved in any unpleasant situations. Remember that problems only get worse if not confronted at the proper time.

"[32]And you shall know the truth, and the truth shall make you free." John 8.32

We must know the truth concerning our condition, sin, our relationship with God and our personal life. For this to happen, someone must be willing to tell us the truth with the purpose of correcting what is wrong in us. This person should be a friend, our pastor, a family member, or a brother who loves us enough to confront us with the truth in love. **The truth by itself really hurts, but if we say it accompanied by love and mercy, it produces the desired effects. We should never confront in anger or with sarcasm because this blocks the communication process.**

Why are some people unable to confront?

Fear of losing a friendship – Sometimes we are fearful of losing the love or friendship of those around us. However, keep in mind that if a person is not confronted, it's because he is not loved enough. Eventually, we will be partially responsible for his fall, because we were aware of his mistakes, or "his blind spot", yet we did nothing to warn him of the danger at the proper time.

Fear of rejection – One main reason we do not confront is the fear of rejection. We want to feel like we belong and fear being kicked out of the group. Also, we lack the courage to confront because we love ourselves. We want to avoid feeling the pain of rejection, or want to avoid loosing a friendship or relationship. The decision not to confront contributes to what is wrong in the person needing confrontation.

The following is a biblical example of confrontation: Peter had a problem and Paul confronted him.

Who was being confronted? Peter. Who confronted him? Paul. What was Peter's problem? His problem was hypocrisy.

"[11]Now when Peter had come to Antioch, I withstood him to his face, because he was to be blamed; [12]for before certain men came from James, he would eat with the Gentiles; but when they came, he withdrew and separated himself, fearing those who were of the circumcision. [13]And the rest of the Jews also played the hypocrite with him, so that even Barnabas was carried away with their hypocrisy. [14]But when I saw that they were not straightforward about the truth of the gospel, I said to Peter before them all, "If you, being a Jew, live in the manner of Gentiles and not as the Jews, why do you compel Gentiles to live as Jews?" Galatians 2.11-14

The Apostle Peter had a problem with hypocrisy. He ate and lived like the Gentiles who lived under grace, trying to convert them to Judaism, yet was afraid to be seen eating with them, by the Jews, who lived under the law of circumcision.

What was the final outcome? Peter repented of his hypocrisy and corrected the problem. Someone loved him enough to confront him with the truth. What was Peter's truth? The truth was that he was acting like a hypocrite, but God took hold of the situation and used Paul to confront him with the truth. As leaders, you must confront continually, as this is a way to grow spiritually.

Steps in order to confront effectively.

We should follow the same steps our Lord used to confront the churches in the book of Revelation. There were several problems in these churches and the Lord confronted them with the truth. Let us take a look at the steps Jesus used to confront effectively.

1. **Begin with an affirmation**. When the confrontation begins with an affirmation it eliminates tension and brings peace between the parties involved. Let us take a look at the following biblical example:

   "2I know your works, your labor, your patience, and that you cannot bear those who are evil. And you have tested those who say they are apostles and are not, and have found them liars; 3and you have persevered and have patience, and have labored for My name's sake and have not become weary." Revelation 2.2,3

   In this verse, it is clear how the Lord confronts the church in Ephesus. He begins by affirming their work, patience, holiness, suffering, and their steadfastness. In the same way, one must confront using phrases such as, "I appreciate and love you because you are generous with me." The most effective method for a successful confrontation is to begin with affirmation. Other sincere phrases such as: "I consider you to be loyal and faithful to me," should also be used.

2. **Express your feelings.** Tell the person you are confronting what bothers you, how you feel, what he did wrong; tell him what you have against him and why.

   "4Nevertheless I have this against you, that you have left your first love." Revelation 2.4

   Use phrases such as: "I feel betrayed," "I have something against you I can't forgive," and "I feel you have not been transparent with me." Be clear and specific. Remember to separate the person from the bad action. You are confronting the person and making them responsible for their actions.

3. **Remind the person when and where he failed you.**

   ***"5Remember therefore from where you have fallen**; repent and do the first works, or else I will come to you quickly and remove your lampstand from its place--unless you repent."* Revelation 2.5

You may use phrases such as, "This misunderstanding occurred when we began working together." "This offense touched my heart when you spoke to another person at work behind my back." "This situation began when you started working in another ministry." The key to reminding them of the problem consists in telling the individual when and where the problem started; it is very important for people to know this. If they are able to understand this, they will be willing to correct their mistakes.

4. **Provide a solution to the problem. "Repent and do the first works."** Jesus provides the solution to correct the problem of their having left their first love. What is the solution? Repent and do the first works.

   Many people constantly talk about a problem without offering solutions, such as these: "I believe that if you acknowledge what you said about me and never do it again…" "It is necessary for you to forgive the offence you suffered", "if you separate yourself from those people and their bad influences…," "if you stop listening to those who don't love me…," "if you leave that sin behind and confess it…," "if you get rid of the anger in your heart, you will be healed." These are only a few suggestions of solutions we can give to the people we are confronting.

5. **Confront immediately; don't wait any longer.** The longer we wait to confront, the less we'll want to do it. Don't wait too long! Do it as soon as possible and stop the enemy from gaining the upper hand!

   "5Or else I will come to you quickly." Revelation 2.5. Jesus gives an ultimatum with the understanding that the church in Ephesus must change the situation immediately. We must confront as soon as possible!

6. **We must be sure there's no anger in us before confronting anyone.** Otherwise, we will hurt the other person and make the situation

worse. Be wise, wait until the anger is gone and then confront the problem.

7. **Talk about the consequences.** When a person is confronted, he must know there is a solution to the situation at hand, but if he doesn't make an effort to solve it, there will be consequences. We must inform him that if he corrects the problem, there won't be any need to face the consequences.

   "[5]Remember therefore from where you have fallen; repent and do the first works, or else ***I will come to you quickly and remove your lampstand from its place****--unless you repent." Revelation 2.5*

   If Jesus spoke of removing His presence from the church in Ephesus if they don't repent of their sin, after losing their first love, then this means there are irreversible consequences for the things we do. We may confront people using phrases such as these: "If you don't stop gossiping, harm will come to your home." "If you don't stop watching those obscene movies, your children will be affected by them." "If you don't tell the truth, you will lose my trust." "If you continue to listen to those who speak ill of me, you will lose my friendship." "If you continue in sin, you will lose the anointing." "If you continue with that friendship, you will be greatly affected." It is extremely important for the person being confronted to understand the consequences of not correcting the problem.

8. **Finish with words of affirmation and reward.** ***"To him who overcomes I will give to eat from the tree of life."*** When Jesus confronted the church at Ephesus, He started and ended with words of affirmation, saying: "If you repent and fix the problem, you will receive the reward." We can use phrases such as: "If we can settle our differences, our friendship will improve." "If you stop your rebellious attitude, we can work better as a team," and so on. It is important to inform the other person of the rewards that come from maintaining a good relationship. Just as we remind them of the consequences, we must also remind him of the rewards in order to enrich his faith.

If you're the one being confronted:

Take responsibility for your actions: ***"[5]unless you repent."*** Recognize your part in the problem; don't blame others because this makes matters worse. Learn to take responsibility for your actions, saying: "Yes, I recognize I said this about you." "Yes, I humble myself for having acted in such an arrogant way." "Yes, I was the one who said those things to that sister." "Yes, I was the one who decided that." Take responsibility for your actions. Do not be afraid of telling the truth for fear of being rejected. If you tell the truth, God will be your judge and your lawyer; He will fight for you.

The following are a few words and attitudes we must avoid when confronting:

Avoid words such as, "never" and "always." Sometimes these words make people fall away and protect themselves, and they don't offer any hope for change. For example: "You never ask for forgiveness." "You are always complaining and murmuring."

Avoid sarcasm. Sarcasm is counter-productive and very offensive. It ignites anger in the other person. It is also an indication that you are more angry with the person than with their actions. Sarcasm uses many ironic and indirect phrases that hurt people.

Confront in private, not in public. Make every effort to confront in private; this avoids causing shame to the other person.

Don't apologize for the confrontation. If we apologize, we give the impression of not knowing what we're doing.

An effective leader must learn how to confront difficult situations in every area and he must have a positive attitude. He must confront every situation with love and courage.

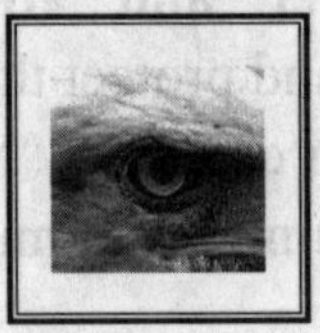

CHAPTER VI

How to Disciple Other People

There is a saying that refers to success in the following way: "Success without a successor is failure." For years, the church has had a shortage of mentors with the ability to disciple others. Jesus gave us the great commission of making disciples throughout the nations; unfortunately, this is not being done. There are many factors that have prevented the great commission of going and making disciples from being accomplished efficiently.

"[19]Go therefore and make disciples of all the nations, baptizing them in the name of the Father and of the Son and of the Holy Spirit." Matthew 28.19

What reasons prevent leaders from being able to reproduce themselves in others?

- **Ignorance.** The leader has no idea how to disciple others nor does he have the desire to learn or find out how to do it. Another reason may be the absence of a role model worthy of imitating and then doing the same with others.

- **Lack of Identity.** It is not knowing who one is in God; it is not having a clear idea of one's calling or position, so much so that, when one of his subordinates rises up with more anointing and charisma, the leader who lacks identity feels threatened and offended. He then chooses not to disciple anyone because he is fearful of losing his position or job. When a leader is sure of his identity, he reproduces himself in others effectively.

  "[12] For though by this time you ought to be teachers, you need someone to teach you again the first principles of the oracles of God; and

you have come to need milk and not solid food. [13]For everyone who partakes only of milk is unskilled in the word of righteousness, for he is a babe. [14]But solid food belongs to those who are of full age, that is, those who by reason of use have their senses exercised to discern both good and evil." Hebrews 5.12-14

- **Fear of delegation.** We believe this is a chain reaction. The root of insecurity is caused by fear, resulting in an inability of people to reproduce themselves effectively. Fear of delegation is one of the reasons leaders choose not to pass on to others what they possess. When we delegate, we give other people the authority to do the same things we do. Sometimes, we choose not to delegate because we are under the impression that the other person is not ready to do a good job, or we think he might abuse the authority that is given to him. Also, we might feel threatened that he might surpass us in authority until finally taking over our position.

- **Lack of a role model.** As leaders, we tend to reproduce ourselves according to our kind, unless we didn't have a mentor or father who took us by the hand and helped us grow. Then we have no example or guide to show us how to reproduce ourselves in others.

- **Lack of a father's heart.** An essential characteristic of a mentor is having the heart of a father. A father doesn't want to shine himself, but rather desires to see his children grow and multiply. One of the biggest problems in the body of Christ today, is the lack of true fathers in the Lord, thus creating a shortage of disciples.

What is the biblical method used to disciple?

There are two teaching schools for disciples, the Greek school and the Hebrew school. These schools observe the following methods:

Greek School	Hebrew School
• The student's role model is the class.	• The student's role model is the mentor.
• It uses the academic method. The studen t and mentor do not have a relationship.	• It uses the relational method based on covenant relationships.
• It is a passive method without application.	• It is an experimental, practical method.
• It is a method based on theory.	• It is a method based on theory.
• Only the teacher participates. • It is a method based on training and capacitation.	• Only the teacher participates. • The teacher and student interact.

Unfortunately, the Greek school still has great influence in our universities, schools and churches. Its influence was so great that humanism and intellectualism became a part of it, thus losing the supernatural and the covenant relationships between mentors and their disciples.

What was the method Jesus used?

Jesus used the Hebrew method. Above all things, He was a role model to His disciples. Let us take a look at one example in the life of Jesus:

"[13]And He went up on the mountain and called to Him those He Himself wanted. And they came to Him. [14]Then He appointed twelve, that they might be with Him and that He might send them out to preach." Mark 3.13,14

In this verse, we see how Jesus had a direct, intimate relationship with His disciples: *"…that they might be with Him…"* He wanted them to be near Him in order to teach them and so that they could experience His teaching for themselves; He equipped them and then sent them out: *"that He might send them out to preach."* This was not only a mental teaching, but a practical one.

The only way for us to disciple those around us, and at the same time, make an impact on their lives, is through covenant relationships.

Leaders can disciple in two ways:

- **A discipleship based on sight and words.** In this type of discipleship, people see the mentor as their role model and follow him; They hear what he says and apply it. The mentor is able to exert a certain level of influence on his disciples without the benefits of a close relationship with him.

- **Discipleship through relationship.** This type of discipleship gathers people under the mentor's wings. Through it, the mentor gives everything he has and the disciples open their hearts. This develops into a close relationship between mentor and disciple, as was the case of Jesus and John.

  "25 Then, leaning back on Jesus' breast, he said to Him, 'Lord, who is it?'" John 13.25

  To lean on Jesus' breast is indicative of a close relationship between the mentor and his disciple; this was the reason Jesus was able to impact their lives the way He did. We can conclude that the biblical method, and the most effective to disciple others and cause great impact, is through the development of covenant relationships. It was previously mentioned that there is a shortage of fathers in the body of Christ. Therefore, it is important to keep in mind that a father is a mentor who desires to disciple others.

What is a mentor?

A mentor has the ability to identify and develop the potential in others through the investment of his gifts, abilities and talents, while leading the disciple to fulfill his destiny. Mentors are individuals with great experience and who enjoy rich, an intimate relationship with God. The word "mentor" in the Greek language means counselor or wise man.

One characteristic of a true mentor is the gift of wisdom in his life; thus making him into the kind of mentor people choose to follow. Another biblical definition for mentor is one who has the wisdom to identify leaders, to discover their potential and to develop them. His desire is to reproduce himself in them with the purpose of sending them out to do the same with others.

What is a disciple?

Disciple is the Greek word *"mathetes,"* meaning apprentice, pupil, one who follows after, one who imitates, a follower. A man is called a *"mathetes"* when he binds himself to someone else to acquire theoretical and practical knowledge. The word disciple means one who places himself under the instruction, teaching and training of a mentor with the purpose of developing his potential.

The most effective way to form, shape and train a disciple is through a close relationship. Commitment is the key to maintaining this relationship between the mentor and the disciple.

What is the mentor's commitment to the disciple?

- The mentor is committed to the **individual.** Every mentor must understand that his first commitment is to the person, accepting him just as he is. How do we show our commitment? When we take care of him, affirm him, and when we show love, not only to him, but to his family as well.

- The mentor must be committed to the process and the **training.** During this time, the disciple will, without a doubt, fail, make mistakes, and at times, break his promises. This is the mentor's opportunity to guide and give him another chance. Teach your disciples that there is no such thing as failure in the Lord, rather, these are lessons from which to learn. At times, the disciple's training process may be hard and painful, not only for the disciple, but for the mentor as well, but as long as they are fully committed to each other, they will survive the process. The mentor's way of thinking is that it doesn't matter how many times he fails, this individual has potential and it can be developed.

- The mentor must be committed to the **calling** or potential in his disciple. The mentor must help identify the calling in his disciple and develop him, providing places and circumstances in which he can grow, until finally, leading him to God's destiny for his life.

What is the disciple's commitment to his mentor?

- **Faithfulness to his mentor.** The word **faithful** is defined as one who does his job consistently without fainting. He can be depended upon, and is committed to the task and the work assigned to him by the mentor.

- **Loyalty to his mentor.** The word **loyal** is defined as one who is committed to his mentor; one who will not abandon him in times of crisis. He is also one who can be trusted and is always available to work. Faithfulness has to do with being consistent in the assigned task, but loyalty is being faithful to the person who assigned the task (the mentor or employer, among others).

- **The disciple must be committed to the process and development of his potential.** The discipleship process includes many things. He must be totally committed to his mentor and complete his assigned tasks, obeying the mentor regardless of what is asked of him.

What process should a believer go through in discipleship?

- **Self-denial.** This expression means a disciple must be willing to leave things behind, and deny his own desires and dreams to do the will of God.

"[34]When He had called the people to Himself, with His disciples also, He said to them, 'Whoever desires to come after Me, let him deny himself, and take up his cross, and follow Me. [35]For whoever desires to save his life will lose it, but whoever loses his life for My sake and the gospel's will save it. [36]For what will it profit a man if he gains the whole world, and loses his own soul'" Mark 8.34-36

- **Leave his old mentality behind.** Every person that enters into the kingdom of God's discipleship must change his old mentality and acquire the mind of Christ.

  "[5]Let this mind be in you which was also in Christ Jesus." Philippians 2.5

- **Take up your cross daily.** This expression, "Take up your cross" means to be ready to die, which is only possible when we deny ourselves; it consists of being truly free of our ego and other forms of personal security. To deny ourselves can only be accomplished when a man totally surrenders himself to an unconditional discipleship.

  "[34]When He had called the people to Himself, with His disciples also, He said to them, 'Whoever desires to come after Me, let him deny himself, and take up his cross, and follow Me'." Mark 8.34

If we were to summarize the work of a mentor and the function of a disciple, we could conclude that each should be committed to the other; this is to say, the mentor to the disciple, as a person, to the process and to the calling. At the same time, the disciple must be committed in faithfulness and loyalty to his mentor; he must also be committed to the training and the process of his calling.

What are the characteristics of a good mentor?

1. **He has the ability to initiate dialogue.** The mentor gives direction to his relationship with his disciples; he takes responsibility for the

health of that relationship and begins the communication process with humility. The mentor initiates this by asking his disciple questions concerning his calling and how he feels about it, his family and more. The mentor is the one who initiates this close relationship.

2. **He is a role model of integrity.** The mentor is not afraid of anyone finding out anything regarding his private life; he is transparent. He is not ashamed of his life when others are not looking, and he reflects the life of Christ in his words and deeds.

3. **A good mentor knows his own identity.** One reason mentors are insecure is that they don't know who they are in Christ. They are afraid of losing their position. Others feel threatened when they see the anointing and the gifts of other people. A good mentor knows his identity in Christ, who called him, and what his calling is. He is mature enough to understand that each time he reproduces himself in others, his anointing increases.

4. **A good mentor has a close relationship with God.** We impart to the people what we know about God. If we have a close relationship with the Lord, we will be able to impart to the disciples His life, peace and joy. Our relationship with God should always resemble that of a good, effective mentor.

5. **A good mentor must be wise.**

   "[13]The fear of the LORD is to hate evil; pride and arrogance and the evil way and the perverse mouth I hate." Proverbs 8.13

   What is wisdom?

   Wisdom is a virtue of the character of God; it consists of knowing the nature of all created things, visible or invisible, and how to deal with them accordingly, and at the opportune time. The most evident virtue in a mature mentor is wisdom to know the origin of all things, the "why" of all things, and how to deal with them. A good mentor must ask for wisdom to deal with people, their motivations and intentions, to use money wisely and to make decisions that benefit the people and please God.

6. **A good mentor affirms his disciples.** Negative attitudes are easily seen in people today, but a good mentor continually affirms his disciples with words and with physical touch. These gestures are desired and yearned for by many.

   What areas should a mentor affirm in his disciples?

   - Affirm him in the area of his personal identity. This has much to do with who the disciple is in Christ. For example: "I can do all things through Christ." "You are God's son or daughter." "You are seated in heavenly places." "Nothing is impossible for you." "You are loved and appreciated by God," and so on. There must always be words of affirmation for your disciples.

   - Affirm him in his work. When one of your disciples does a good job in whatever was entrusted to him, affirm him verbally, in public and in private. Use expressions such as: "Good job, I am so proud of you." "You did that with excellence." "You are a good disciple," and so on.

   - Affirm him in his calling in Christ. Some disciples need to hear from their mentors and be affirmed in their calling in Christ to increase their confidence in what they are doing.

7. **A good mentor is continually growing spiritually.** A mentor is unable to take his disciples to another level of growth, unless he has been there first. It is crucial for the mentor to read all the time, attend conferences, learn from other men and associate with people who have greater anointing and wisdom; these help him to grow spiritually and personally. Never follow a mentor that has stopped growing in God.

How should you disciple others?

To learn how to disciple others, we will use, as a reference, the method Jesus used with his twelve disciples; He is the perfect mentor.

1. **Jesus was their teacher (He brought revelation).**

   The first thing Jesus did was to teach. It is impossible for anyone to do a job unless he is first taught, instructed or until he receives the impartation of the theory. Teaching and practicing go together; it must go from theory to application. Jesus revealed new biblical truths that challenged His leadership.

   "[1]And seeing the multitudes, He went up on a mountain, and when He was seated His disciples came to Him. [2]Then He opened His mouth and taught them, saying:" Matthew 5.1, 2

   Jesus taught his disciples and gave them instructions before sending them out; He showed them what to do before asking them to do it. As mentors, we should never ask our disciples to do what we have not taught them or what they have not seen us do.

2. **Jesus demonstrated what He taught. (He gave a demonstration.)**

   He gave them a visible demonstration of what He was teaching.

   "[26]And when the disciples saw Him walking on the sea, they were troubled, saying, 'It is a ghost!' And they cried out for fear. [27]But immediately Jesus spoke to them, saying, 'Be of good cheer! It is I; do not be afraid'." Matthew 14. 26-27

   Jesus walked on water. First, Jesus taught them to live by faith and believe in God; then, He showed them. It is crucial to teach our disciples, and then demonstrate what we teach, whether it is character, gifts, miracles, leadership or anything else. Each time a mentor teaches something to his disciples, he must demonstrate what he is teaching immediately. **For the most part, disciples learn more when they see it done, than when they merely hear it taught**.

3. Jesus imparted (He transferred everything he had.)

Through the laying on of hands or the spoken Word, Jesus imparted to His disciples what He had, and transferred the anointing and the power that ran through Him.

"[1]Then He called His twelve disciples together and gave them power and authority over all demons, and to cure diseases. [2]He sent them to preach the kingdom of God and to heal the sick." Luke 9.1, 2

This is when the mentor must transfer what he has to his disciple and it must be done through the laying on of hands.

4. Jesus activated His disciples (activation):

"[12]So they went out and preached that people should repent. [13]And they cast out many demons, and anointed with oil many who were sick, and healed them." Mark 6.12, 13

In this example, the Apostle Paul learned from Jesus how to activate and stir up the gifts in the disciples.

What is activation?

Activation means to challenge the disciples to live or walk in the truth they have just received, to receive the grace to act it out and live it. Activation has to do with awakening the gifts and talents that are dormant in the disciples; mentors have the ability to activate the gifts within them. Every time a mentor teaches, demonstrates or imparts a truth, he must also activate each of his disciples, that they may receive the grace of God and practice what they have just received.

5. **Jesus sends them out to be multiplied (mobilized).**

   "[7]And He called the twelve to Himself, and began to send them out two by two, and gave them power over unclean spirits." Mark 6.7

   This is a very important part of the process. At this time, the disciple is given authority and the power to reproduce himself in others, duplicating his own experience. If we were to condense the five steps on how Jesus took His twelve disciples through the discipleship process, we could say the following: Jesus brought **revelation** or taught new biblical truths. He gave them a visible **demonstration** of what He was teaching and **imparted to them** what He had through the laying on of hands. He **activated** them, prayed for God's grace over them and the ability to do the same things He did. And last of all, He sent them to multiply themselves and **mobilized** them to do the same.

Steps to identify potential disciples.

"[2]And the things that you have heard from me among many witnesses, commit these to faithful men who will be able to teach others also." 2 Timothy 2.2

The first thing we must do before choosing potential disciples in whom we will invest our lives into, is to know the essential steps of how to identify and choose them. What was the first thing Jesus did prior to choosing His apostles?

The first thing Jesus did was pray:

"[12]Now it came to pass in those days that He went out to the mountain to pray, and continued all night in prayer to God. [13]And when it was day, He called His disciples to Himself; and from them He chose twelve whom He also named apostles." Luke 6.12,13

Every mentor must keep in mind that he will choose the wrong people if he doesn't pray about it first. If he chooses without praying about it, his disciples will be people without the ability to multiply themselves in others. If this happens, the mentor will realize, too late, that he wasted his time. One important thing to keep in mind is that mentors seek and choose their disciples, not the other way around. Such was the case of Jesus; He was the one who sought after His disciples.

What are some characteristics to look for in potential disciples?

The person to be chosen for discipleship must be:

- **Faithful.** This individual does his job consistently. He is trustworthy and dependable; he will not abandon his assigned tasks.

- **Available.** Some disciples may fill every requirement, they are faithful and good, but they do not have the time available to comply with what is required in a discipleship.

- **The disciple must have a teachable spirit.** It is very difficult for a mentor to disciple someone who is constantly questioning and debating what he is taught. A disciple must be willing to change the old mentality and have a teachable spirit.

- **The disciple must be hungry for growth.** This is a very important point, because if the disciple doesn't hunger for growth, he will not receive the teachings with joy or be able to rise to other levels.

- **Potential gifts.** The disciple must have potential gifts that are clearly seen and easily developed for leadership.

How should we begin the discipleship process?

As you take the initiative and begin praying to the Lord to give you the right people, there are a few steps that should be taken:

1. **Gather the disciples and establish the vision.** Discipleship is not socializing or building new friendships. Although this is part of it, it is not the objective. Discipleship is a time to come together to be trained, equipped and finally sent out. Later, these disciples are to multiply themselves in others; to do this they must have vision and conviction.

2. **Select and determine the number of disciples.** Select the individual or people to be your disciple(s). Take all the time you need to relate to them. In this way, your wise investment will bring great dividends to the kingdom or your company. It is advisable that the group not be greater than thirty people. Otherwise, the relationship between mentor and disciple may be lost.

3. **Convey the vision of multiplication.** The reason for discipleship must be specified. Explain your desire to see them multiply and do the same in others. Explain the context of the training, what the discipleship entails, not only as a person, but also, at the ministerial level.

4. **Request a commitment.** To enter discipleship is a blessing. Therefore, the disciple must be committed to the process and to the mentor. The commitment of the disciple includes being on time to all the meetings and to support financially, spiritually and emotionally, the discipleship classes and the mentor.

5. **Meet as often as possible.** During these sessions, give the disciples lessons they can write down and participate in. Remember this is an intensive discipleship; the teacher speaks and the students are given the opportunity to ask questions. There should be mutual

communication during the teachings. I suggest you meet once a week or twice a month. Each meeting should last approximately 2 hours.

6. **Every time you teach something, activate your disciples.** Activation is extremely important. Through it, the mentor is able to impart of his spirit to the disciples, and thus, stir up their gifts. (It is extremely important that the disciples receive the mentor's spirit.)

7. **Set goals and times for the discipleship.** Evaluate the disciples, set goals, and make sure they know how long the discipleship will take. For example, our personal discipleship is between two to three years.

8. **Send them.** The goal of discipleship should not be to keep them for ourselves, but to send them out to multiply themselves in others.

"14Then He appointed twelve, that they might be with Him and that He might send them out to preach." Mark 3.14

What should we teach the disciples?

- **Christian fundamentals.** A reason many disciples drop out of the discipleship process is the type of foundation they have. We must give them a good foundation before placing more bricks on their structure. Biblical fundamentals include: faith, baptism, repentance of dead works, the second coming of Jesus Christ, eternal judgment, prayer, the Lord's Supper, fasting, the blood of Jesus, justification, salvation, and others. If every disciple is given a good foundation, as he grows into a "building", he will be solid and indestructible.

- **Charisma.** During this stage of the ministry, the disciple is taught how to discover his gifts, given a place to develop them and he receives help reaching his destiny. It includes spiritual gifts, how to know the calling of God on his life, and the complete study of each gift. Also, the preparation and separation required to accomplish the calling, ministerial gifts, the gifts of the Holy Spirit, motivational gifts, ministerial ethics, the anointing and how to follow its leading, how to flow in the supernatural, inner healing and deliverance.

- **Character.** This is the most important step for a disciple. It is pointless for the disciple to have excellent charisma if he has poor character; because it will cause his ministry to fall. What topics are included in the discipleship of character? Integrity, honesty, motives, moral values, beatitudes, faithfulness, submission, holiness, spiritual maturity, the fruits of the Spirit, fear of God, obedience and respect.

- **Leadership.** In this area of leadership the following topics will be taught: What is a leader; How to become a leader; how to disciple others; the profile of a leader; the characteristics of a leader; the vision of the church; and more.

- **Deliverance** and inner healing. It is important to minister deliverance and inner healing to every leader or disciple. Before teaching him, you must cleanse him. Otherwise, he will not be ready to receive knowledge. Wounds and demonic influence in an individual inhibit him from freely receiving knowledge from the Word of God. Dear mentor, do not begin your discipleship without first ministering deliverance and inner healing to your disciples; and finally, teach them this principle so that they can do the same with their disciples.

- **Devotional life.** Prayer, how to develop a constant and powerful prayer life, how to study the Word, intercession and spiritual warfare. The devotional life of a leader can be summed up in having a close relationship with God, by talking to Him in prayer and reading His Word.

- **The Family.** Marriage, raising children, roles and functions in the home, communication, sex in marriage, attitudes and actions that destroy the family, single, but satisfied. Keep in mind that a leader is as strong as his family life is.

- **Evangelism.** How to evangelize in a supernatural way and biblical gifts needed to disciple others in evangelism. Every disciple must be trained and equipped in the area of evangelism. Disciples must be taught to love the lost and they must be trained on how to win the lost.

- **Covenant relationships.** What is a covenant? Entering into a covenant relationship with God, yourself, your family, the church and the pastor. The kingdom of God is established through close relationships. These have two directions: vertical, with God, and horizontally, with men. The mentor must be sure the disciple is molded in all areas of life, to become a man or woman of God ready for every good work.

"15Be diligent to present yourself approved to God, a worker who does not need to be ashamed, rightly dividing the word of truth." 2 Timothy 2.15

- **Evangelism:** How to evangelize in a supernatural way and biblical gifts needed to disciple others in evangelism. Every disciple must be trained and equipped in the area of evangelism. Disciples must be taught to love the lost and they must be trained on how to win the lost.

- **Covenant relationships:** What is a covenant? Entering into a covenant relationship with God yourself, your family, the church and the pastor. The kingdom of God is established through close relationships. These have two directions: vertical, with God, and horizontally with men. The mentor must be sure the disciple is molded in all areas of life, to become a man or woman of God ready for every good work.

"Be diligent to present yourself approved to God, a worker who does not need to be ashamed, rightly dividing the word of truth." 2 Timothy 2:15

CHAPTER VII

The Art of Delegating Authority

One facet of leadership is the ability to delegate responsibilities to potential disciples. Unfortunately, there are many leaders who make mistakes when delegating. As a result, leaders are not reproducing themselves. To delegate is an art form. We learn to trust others through this process. At times, we might think there is nobody else capable of doing the job better than we are, but it is necessary to delegate and trust our disciples, even when it is understood that they will be making mistakes. This is all part of the process.

"[25]And Moses chose able men out of all Israel, and made them heads over the people: rulers of thousands, rulers of hundreds, rulers of fifties, and rulers of tens. [26]So they judged the people at all times; the hard cases they brought to Moses, but they judged every small case themselves." Exodus 18.25,26

The following steps should be followed before delegating to others:

1. **Selection :**

   This is the process whereby potential disciples, those we think capable of doing the task at hand, should be brought together. When the moment comes to make this selection, it is important to pray and ask God who the right people are. They should not be chosen for their physical appearance or their intellectual abilities, but with God's guidance.

   "[16]So the LORD said to Moses: "Gather to Me seventy men of the elders of Israel." Numbers 11.16

2. Disciples must meet the following prerequisites:

- People should recognize the disciples. When the people know them, it makes the job a lot easier.

"[21]Moreover you shall select from all the people able men, such as fear God, men of truth, hating covetousness; and place such over them to be rulers of thousands, rulers of hundreds, rulers of fifties, and rulers of tens." Exodus 18.21

- They are fearful of God. Disciples do what pleases God; they keep away from sin, love what is good, hate what is evil and practice holiness.

- They are virtuous. They have a good testimony before God and the people. No one is able to point fingers at them because of poor conduct within the church, or on the outside.

- They are honest. They walk in integrity, their conduct is consistent and their words complement their actions.

- They do not covet. These are men and women with pure intentions; they do not love money.

Once these people are selected, we must make sure they meet certain prerequisites before delegating anything to them.

What are we going to delegate?

Authority – the word authority means the delegated legal right to execute dominion; it is backed up by power.

"[19]Behold, I give you the authority to trample on serpents and scorpions, and over all the power of the enemy, and nothing shall by any means hurt you." Luke 10.19

Every person delegating authority must know what he is giving the disciple, which is the legal right to act in his name, in the name of his business, ministry or organization. This legal right or authority must be given in private, as well as in public, for the people to follow him.

Once authority has been delegated, it can't be taken away unless there is rebellion.

Sometimes, as leaders, we may feel tempted to remove this authority when the disciple doesn't do things exactly as we do. This is the perfect opportunity for us to understand that these disciples are bound to make mistakes and that we should be committed to the learning process.

All delegated authority is based on submission.

"7Therefore submit to God. Resist the devil and he will flee from you." James 4.7

The level of authority we receive is based on the level of submission we have towards God first, and second, our leader. Leaders that are unable to submit should not command orders because they do not obey authority.

- **Responsibility** – Delegated authority and responsibility go together, implying that a person has a job to do and is committed to see it through. Many people desire authority without responsibility, but when a level of authority is delegated to us, it brings with it a certain level of responsibility equivalent to it. When the mentor delegates authority and responsibility to his disciple, it means he is expecting the disciple to be responsible.

A few important aspects:

- Delegating authority according to the disposition and **ability** of the disciple. If the disciple's ability is to lead ten people, then don't give him authority to lead one hundred.

- Delegate according to the **gift or passion** of the disciple; he must be placed in the proper position. God gave us each a gift. Disciples should be placed according to the passion and talent he possesses. A job should never be assigned to an individual if he doesn't have the passion to see it through. Rather, he must be placed in areas of service that complement his calling or passion.

What did Jesus do when He delegated authority to His disciples?

- **He gave specific instructions** – This is a very important point to understand. Many times disciples are unable to fulfill their responsibilities because they are not given specific instructions (how, when, what, where, and why) as to what the job consists of. Giving specific instructions prevents future problems.

"5These twelve Jesus sent out and commanded them, saying: 'Do not go into the way of the Gentiles, and do not enter a city of the Samaritans. 6But go rather to the lost sheep of the house of Israel. 7And as you go, preach, saying, 'The kingdom of heaven is at hand.' 8Heal the sick, cleanse the lepers, raise the dead, cast out demons. Freely you have received, freely give'." Matthew 10.5-8

One principle of the process of delegating that we should know is:

- Every time we delegate authority, there is transference of spirit. This means that God is imparting from the leader's spirit into the disciple.

"17Then I will come down and talk with you there. I will take of the Spirit that is upon you and will put the same upon them; and they shall bear the burden of the people with you, that you may not bear it yourself alone." Numbers 11.17

The disciple should be aware of the following biblical principals:

- **Be accountable.** Once the disciple is entrusted with authority and responsibility, he should give detailed reports of his work.

*"[17]Then **the seventy returned** with joy, saying, "Lord, even the demons are subject to us in Your name." Luke 10.17*

This passage teaches us that, after the Lord delegated authority and responsibility to His disciples, they returned with a report of everything He asked them to do. A good disciple is accountable for his actions.

- **Disciples must understand that responsibility and authority are delegated.** These should not be abused. Many leaders abuse their authority, manipulate and control the people to the point of hurting them. The disciple's authority is based on submission and a healthy relationship with his leader. If he rebels against the leader, all authority given to him should be taken away immediately. Rebellion cannot be allowed under any circumstances.

- **The disciple's first commitment is to serve with the purpose of alleviating the leader's burden.** The authority received by the disciple is to serve the people and not to satisfy his own interests.

"[17]They shall bear the burden of the people with you, that you may not bear it yourself alone." Numbers 11.17

- **Faithfulness and loyalty belongs to God first, then the leader.** This is a quality in the character of a good disciple. Loyalty is important in business, inside and outside the church, the home and everywhere else.

- **Maintain a teachable heart and a willingness to be disciplined.** When you make a mistake, accept the correction.

TEST
How to Delegate Correctly

1	Authority is delegated to a subordinate with experience in similar jobs.	F	T
2	The person to whom you delegate authority must have all the information or teaching on the job he is delegated to do.	F	T
3	It must be established, from the beginning, the boundaries of the work that is delegated.	F	T
4	In any delegated job, the method is as important as the desired result.	F	T
5	Critical decisions involved in doing a job are still considered to be the delegator's domain.	F	T
6	The person delegating authority must always be clear to the one receiving it, that the job or labor he is about to do, is a challenge, regardless of how simple it is.	F	T
7	Delegating means to transfer authority from one person to another, for a specific job.	F	T
8	Advice or complete information should be given to the disciples when authority is delegated.	F	T
9	The same standard of accountability should be given to all the disciples, when the mentor delegates authority.	F	T
10	If the disciple fails at the job he was delegated to do, he should be given a second chance.	F	T

Answers: 1)F 2)T 3)T 4)F 5)F 6)F 7)T 8)T 9)F 10)T

CHAPTER VIII

The Price of Being an Anointed Leader

The glory, the distinction, or the benefits of the anointing should never be the motivation of someone who aspires to be a leader. Sometimes, people see what is going on at the altar, like the anointing, the miracles and the power, to mention just a few. However, they are unaware of the high price that must be paid when God chooses to use you, or what goes on behind the scenes. Once, while studying the subject of the anointing, and before I began writing on how to develop leadership, God asked me, "Are you willing to pay the price?" I answered, "What price?" He responded: "The price of loneliness, peer pressure and circumstances, the price of mental and physical fatigue, of depriving yourself of good things, the price of seeking my face and studying the Word while others sleep and enjoy themselves." A high price is always demanded of the true leader, anointed with the grace and the favor of God. The more effective the leader, the higher the price he has to pay. If we desire to take the challenge of becoming an anointed leader and of making an impact on our generation, we should be ready to pay the price and accept the responsibility that comes with it. Everybody can see the glory behind the leader, but they don't know his story, or the many challenges, trials and difficulties an anointed leader must face, but in this chapter we will study a few of the most common.

Jesus explains this in detail in the book of Matthew.

"25But Jesus called them to Himself and said, "You know that the rulers of the Gentiles lord it over them, and those who are great exercise authority over them. 26Yet it shall not be so among you; but whoever desires to become great among you, let him be your servant. 27And whoever desires to be first among you, let him be your slave-- 28just as the Son of Man did not come to be served, but to serve, and to give His life a ransom for many." Matthew 20.2528

The word **"great"** in the Greek language means someone who wants to be in front, to be a leader with anointing, and he wants to tell others how to lead. Jesus goes on to say, "He will be our servant." The word **"servant"** is the word *"diakono,"* meaning a servant willing to carry or supply the needs of others. Jesus adds, "**Anyone who wants to be first.**" Here, He meant to say that if anyone desires to be a leader with authority, he must first become our servant. The Greek word for servant is "*doulos,*" meaning a permanent slave to others. What was Jesus trying to teach his disciples? He says anyone with the desire to have a leadership position or a special anointing, must first be everybody's servant. He should supply their needs and permanently serve the people. The anointing is not for the purpose of supplying our own desires, but to supply God's desires and the needs of the people. God will not give a special anointing to people without a servant's heart, or if they don't care about the people.

What price must be paid by the anointed leader to serve with God's power and grace, and be used by Him?

1. **Sacrifice and self-denial.** It is demanded of anointed leaders that they commit themselves to serving others and that they place others needs before their own. Anointed leaders, preoccupied with exalting their own desires, objectives and goals are not true leaders. True anointed leaders are willing to sacrifice their personal objectives to help and to serve others.

   "[17]From now on let no one trouble me, for I bear in my body the marks of the Lord Jesus." Galatians 6.17

   "[39]He who finds his life will lose it, and he who loses his life for My sake will find it." Matthew 10.39

   If you were born to be a leader with purpose, you will not be able to escape paying the price of personal sacrifice. Remember that true anointed leaders not only know their purpose and the objective for which they live; they also know the vision for which they are willing to die. You will never change your generation unless you are willing to die for that change. Greatness in life is found in the willingness to die for something. The Apostle Paul speaks to us about the personal sacrifice he had to endure.

"[4]But in all things we commend ourselves as ministers of God: in much patience, in tribulations, in needs, in distresses, [5]in stripes, in imprisonments, in tumults, in labors, in sleeplessness, in fastings; [6]by purity, by knowledge, by longsuffering, by kindness, by the Holy Spirit, by sincere love." 2 Corinthians 6.4-6

2. **Rejection.** One price the anointed leader must pay is to experience being rejected. If you are willing to accept the call of your generation, you should prepare yourselves for being rejected and misunderstood. Every person in this world wants to be accepted and to feel like they belong to something, but to be an anointed leader or a man or woman of God, the price must be paid, first. At times, people will reject you because you are living righteously and in integrity. This lifestyle brings conviction of sin, resulting in opposition and resistance; Jesus had to experience this. True anointed leaders bring change, and this, by nature, causes conflict and resistance.

Why are leaders rejected? Leaders are rejected because they challenge the people to change their life styles. Leaders tell society that God is a holy God, that they should live in righteousness, and that abortion and homosexuality are sins. When they tell believers to stop living in mediocrity and to begin to live a victorious, holy life, people will reject it. They don't appreciate being told what contradicts their thoughts; they don't want to hear that they need to change.

Leaders are God's "Tabanos" or horseflies. This insect bites people while they sleep. During the time the Spaniards came to America, the Indians fought against them. The Indian chief, to protect the village, would leave one of his children keeping watch at night, who at times would fall asleep and stop watching. To prevent them from falling asleep while on duty, he would place a horsefly inside the watchtower. This solved the problem of keeping his son from falling asleep, ensuring that he would remain alert and on guard. Anointed leaders are society's horseflies, especially for believers without vision, or those that serve out of convenience and not commitment; they are casual believers, without purpose. They are carnal, spiritually warm, and lack conviction. God's horseflies encourage the people to change from mediocrity to excellence, in Christ. Rejection doesn't mean you were mistaken, but it does indicate that you are daring others to change. Remember what the word says:

"Blessed are those who are persecuted for my righteousness sake."

No man is totally accepted until he has been completely rejected.

"10Blessed are those who are persecuted for righteousness' sake, for theirs is the kingdom of heaven." Matthew 5.10

Rejection is part of God's plan that leads to success. Anointed leaders who make an impact on their nation will never be able to escape rejection or being misunderstood.

3. **Criticism.** All leaders must identify themselves with this reality; it's a leader's life style. In other words, criticism is the way of life for a leader; he must always know how to handle it. There is not one leader around who has been able to escape it. The greatest proof of maturity, conviction and commitment to his vision in a leader is reflected in his attitude when confronted with criticism. Humility will never be put to the test with greater intensity than at this time. If you are prepared to receive criticism, then you are ready to become leaders. The mere nature of an effective leader entails taking a position on specific topics and making decisions that determine direction and affect many lives. This will almost always result in a negative reaction (criticism and gossip). However, we need to understand that true leaders

are not affected by criticism. In many situations, it will just seem like a good opportunity to prove their conviction and commitment.

If you don't want to be criticized, then you must decide not to do anything in life. It is far better to be criticized for doing something, then to be ignored for lack of action.

"[11]Blessed are you when they revile and persecute you, and say all kinds of evil against you falsely for My sake. [12]Rejoice and be exceedingly glad, for great is your reward in heaven, for so they persecuted the prophets who were before you." Matthew 5.11-12

4. **Loneliness.** A leader is a loner because it means he has to be in front, ahead of his followers. As leaders, the closer we get to God, the lonelier we will be because, as we approach God, He changes, sanctifies and transforms us. Being in His presence changes us. When we apply these ideas to our lives, people begin to look at us funny. They might not understand us, and at times, may even accuse us of being crazy. Why? Because they are not on the same level of prayer, sanctity or revelation. We will feel alone. The loneliest people are those who are entrusted with a message, a dream or a vision. Great leaders, men and women who touched their generations, were the loneliest of souls. The man that depends on people to feel complete and embraced, will find it very difficult to be a leader and to get ahead because this road must be walked alone. This is the price of the anointing. I love people and love sharing with them, but they are not the source of the wholeness I feel; Jesus is the source. He is a living example of this. His disciples abandoned Him during the most critical time of His life. Regardless of this, He fulfilled His purpose.

   If you are not willing to stand alone in the vision, then no one will be willing to stand with you.

5. **Pressure of making right decisions.** Leaders must face the inevitable challenge that comes with demand and responsibility of

leadership. This involves making critical decisions, often under internal and external pressure. Anointed leaders should take all things into consideration (information and opinions), in order to make the best possible decision. This could become a challenge to their emotional, physical and mental ability, and at times, it may become the source of temporary stress if it's not managed correctly. Few followers appreciate what this implies for leaders. They are unaware of the criticism and pressures imposed by people upon leaders. There is a question that arises from this, "Are we trying to please God or man?"

"10For do I now persuade men, or God? Or do I seek to please men? For if I still pleased men, I would not be a bondservant of Christ." Galatians 1.10

6. **Physical, mental and spiritual fatigue.** The demands of leadership are heavy, especially the physical and mental fatigue. It is impossible to be good leaders and remain unaffected by stress, physical and mental fatigue. Sometimes, upon returning from a miracle and healing crusade, God impresses upon me to pray. I am totally exhausted; there is no strength left in me, but it is necessary to pray because God is the One asking me to. I have no choice; I have to do it! If you are willing to work hard, give more of your time, work more intensely, and go beyond your obligations, then you will be effective leaders and the anointing of God will back you up. For this reason, leaders should incorporate into their life styles healthy diet plans. Keep in mind that when a person is physically and mentally exhausted, he is more vulnerable to the temptations of the enemy, who is always waiting for us to be at our most vulnerable moment.

A few suggestions that should be taken into consideration when you feel fatigue:

- Don't make any important decisions. Your mind is not clear enough to reason properly.

- Don't remain alone for long periods of time, in any given place. The enemy might set a trap for you.

- Seek God's presence. It's the best place to be when you want to renew your strength.

7. **The price paid by the leader's family.** If you are willing to pay the price for fatigue, then you are ready to lead. **Anointed leaders should not expect to live normal lives, as others do.** All of your time, your talents, and experience will be used to serve others. This life style has a direct impact on your family (spouse and children) and close friends. Everyone around us will, inevitably, pay the price. The man or woman of God has to carefully balance service and the fulfillment of their responsibilities and family obligations.

CHAPTER IX

Priorities of a Leader

Few leaders know the principles and understand their importance, yet many of them still have no idea how to set their priorities in order.

What is a priority?

Priority is what is most important, beneficial, productive, essential, and whatever is needed the most. When we speak of something as a priority, we are saying it has first place on our list of importance and must be done at the proper time. These things are so important, the outcome of our lives, whether it is good or bad, depends on it. Unfortunately, some leaders don't know how to set their priorities in order. They exchange what is important for something urgent, the best for the good, thinking that because something resembles an emergency, it is the most important thing and this is not necessarily true. We must learn to set our priorities in order. To do this, we must know what they are according to the Lord and His Word.

1. **Our communion and relationship with God.**

   In prior chapters, I wrote about this, but now let us go a little deeper. Why is our communion and relationship with God the most important thing? Our lives are centered on our relationship with Him. It is in our communion with Him that we are changed, strengthened and transformed. It is where He reveals His plans, purpose and desires. It is what we depend on to make every important decision. Communion with God is a priority because our existence and relationship with our neighbor depends on it. If we are not close to God, we will be a failure in every area of our lives.

What does our relationship with God consist of?

- Prayer every day or talking with God. It is telling Him everything that is in our hearts; to speak with the Heavenly Father; to have a dialogue with Him. It is not vain repetition. The Word of God teaches us to pray and not to repeat words in vain. Prayer implies having a close relationship with God.

Why is talking and praying to God, important?

- Prayer gives God the legal right to act here on earth. Everything God does on earth is because someone asked Him to do it.

- Prayer keeps us from temptation.

  "41 Watch and pray, lest you enter into temptation. The spirit indeed is willing, but the flesh is weak." Matthew 26.41

  When we pray to God, He gives us strength to be self-controlled, to be strong and to overcome temptation.

- Prayer develops an intimate communion with God.

  God's desire is to have a family with which to speak, communicate and have communion. He left us the method of prayer through which we can speak with Him. Prayer is a priority because talking with the Heavenly Father, with the Creator of the heavens and earth before leaving our homes, is the most important, essential, beneficial, productive and necessary thing to do. This is more important than our family, employment, business and ministry.

  Let us take a look at Martha's and Mary's example in the Word of God.

"38 Now it happened as they went that He entered a certain village; and a certain woman named Martha welcomed Him into her house. 39 And she had a sister called Mary, who also sat at Jesus'feet and heard His word. 40 But Martha was distracted with much serving, and she approached Him and said, "Lord, do You not care that my sister has left me to serve alone? Therefore tell her to help me." 41 And Jesus answered and said to her, "Martha, Martha, you are worried and troubled about many things. 42 But one thing is needed, and Mary has chosen that good part, which will not be taken away from her." Luke 10.38-42

Here we have two people, sisters living in the same house with different priorities. One is anxious about the daily chores of life, and the other focuses on having an intimate relationship with God. We will now study what Jesus said in regards to giving God priority in our lives.

"39 Mary, who also sat at Jesus' feet and heard His word."

Jesus arrived at their home. According to Hebrew custom, the women received the guests and then retired to the kitchen to prepare the meal. Women were not allowed to be in the living room, especially if the guest was a man.

"40 But Martha was distracted with much serving."

The word **"distracted"** in the Greek language means to crawl around in circles. In reading about the two women, we find Martha worried about the meal and Mary sitting down listening to Jesus. Mary places God first, giving Jesus priority; she did this overlooking tradition which said that the oldest of the two women should be the one to prepare the meal. Mary breaks all of man's traditions and decides to put Jesus first. This same thing happens today. We are so busy with our jobs, business, family, or school, that these things take priority or first place in our lives. We make them out to be the most important thing and neglect our relationship with God. Mary, instead of doing what tradition said she had to do, which was cook for Jesus, she thought to herself and said: "I know that cooking is important, but it is not the most important thing at this moment. Therefore, I will sit down and hear what Jesus has to say."

"41 Martha, you are worried and troubled about many things."

The words "**worried and troubled"** mean to have a divided mind, to doubt and to be without direction. As we can see, the result of anxiety is doubt, unbelief, to go around in circles, to remain in the same place without the ability to move forward. When an individual worries, it is because he does not trust in God, and the number one reason why there is no trust in Him is because there is no communion, no prayer life with the Father; there is no intimacy. Now, Jesus is about to declare what the most important, beneficial, productive, necessary and essential thing is:

"42 But one thing is needed."

What can be called necessary or a priority? It is exactly what Mary was doing, sitting at Jesus' feet, listening to the Word, having communion with Him, listening to Him speak. Talking with Him on a daily basis is the most important thing. Never leave your house unless you pray first. Jesus explains the benefits of giving Him priority in our lives.

"42 Mary has chosen that good part, which will not be taken away from her."

There are two Greek words for the word **"good"**. One is *"kalos,"* meaning something that is pleasing to the eyes. The other word is "*agathos,*" meaning a good thing, something useful for life. Martha did something that was good, ("kalos") something that seemed right at a glance, but not useful for the rest of her life. You can rise in the morning and exercise, prepare breakfast for your children, study, work; but these things are only temporary. Mary, however, did something completely different. She did something good, ("agathos") something that was useful for the rest of her life. What was that? Her close relationship with God, to hear the voice of the master, to hear His Word, to sit by His side, pray, and speak with Him. This is a treasure that can never be taken away. I believe that if we desire to be leaders that conquer and make an impact upon nations, communities and towns, we must have a close relationship with God. He gives us wisdom, vision and strategies to act and to overcome. Before leaving your home in the morning, you must have that communion, intimacy, with the Heavenly Father through His Son, Jesus Christ. Although it is important and necessary to take care of the things that come up daily, they are not, and should never be, the number one priority.

What is the world's priority?

"25 Therefore I say to you, do not worry about your life, what you will eat or what you will drink; nor about your body, what you will put on. Is not life more than food and the body more than clothing?" Matthew 6.25

"32 For after all these things the Gentiles seek. For your heavenly Father knows that you need all these things." Matthew 6.32

Jesus said to the Gentiles, "Those who do not trust in God, trust in their own abilities and contacts." They are self-sufficient; they rely on their diplomas titles and money. They are looking for everything else, things such as: clothes, food, cars and houses. It is God's desire to give us all these things and He will, as long as we seek Him first.

What is the answer to all this?

First, we must seek the things of the kingdom. These are: prayer, the Word of God, worship and praise, joy, peace, righteousness, communion and close relationship with God. Once these are a priority, everything else is added unto us: houses, cars, food, drink, lands and more. Unfortunately, the world is going about it the wrong way. It seeks the things that are to be added first, and then, if there is time, it seeks God.

Most people regard God as a fireman. He is only sought after and called for, when there is an emergency; when the rope is around their necks; when the business is going downhill; when divorce is a certainty; or when they hit rock bottom.

"[5]You shall love the LORD your God with all your heart, with all your soul, and with all your strength." Deuteronomy 6.5

God spoke from ancient times. He said the first commandment is to love God with all our heart and with all our soul. God should be first; He is essential. Seeking Him is the most beneficial thing we can do; it is the most important thing. When we do this, God adds all the things we need to our lives.

2. The family.

An individual's leadership is intimately inter-related with the family. If we have a solid home life, then our ministry, nation and city will be strong and solid. Family problems are reflected in the leader. The Word of God says: "The one who can't govern his own home, can't govern God's things." Family values are in crisis; adultery, fornication, homosexuality and infidelity increase more each day. There is no fear of God. If we desire to be leaders in the twenty-first century, leaders that will have on impact on the world, we must re-establish family values. Unfortunately, children today must look for heroes and role models in famous recording artists and athletes because they lack good role models at home. These same athletes divorce and marry more than once, live in sin, practice homosexuality, are excessive drinkers, use drugs and make lousy role models for our children.

As parents, we must be their example and role model; we should never wait until they look elsewhere. We must make every effort to re-establish family values. How can this be done? The answer to this question is found in the essential keys on how to create a good family atmosphere and how to restore lost family values:

- **The family was constituted under the marriage covenant.**

  Covenants can't be broken or undone because the consequences are serious such as death, misery, pain and broken hearts. Every leader must make every effort to maintain and guard the marriage covenant. He must recognize that dissolving the marriage will unleash serious consequences. But, if he safeguards it, the blessings are great. God established the marriage covenant to spread His name over the face of the earth. I have seen many leaders break this covenant and suffer serious consequences because of it. The results were wounds, emotional and spiritual scars that can never be erased. God forgives us if there is genuine repentance, but the fact remains that these emotional scars will be a part of us forever.

- **Each one of us must know our responsibilities, role and function within the family.**

  One great family problem is that neither side knows what their function is (the man, woman, or children). This causes divorce in the home. In my book, *The Happy Family*, I specifically write about the functions and roles of the man, woman and of the children. When we are clear what our function is, there is order and authority in the home.

- **Invest quality time in your family.**

  One of the love languages in the family is quality time. Unfortunately, we live in a world full of anxiety, rush and worries with **little quality time** for the family. When we decide to spend time with our children or spouse, we should make sure the phone, television, or anything else that can distract us from having quality time with them, is turned off.

- **What is quality time?**

  It is to focus on something in body, soul and spirit. It is not to be distracted or focused on other things. Remember, after God, our family is the most important entity in our lives. It is necessary, productive and essential. If you dedicate quality time to your family, it will be strong and healthy. You should go on vacation once a year, take them out to dinner, play a sport, take them to the park, etc. During these times with your family, nothing should distract you. Your family is our most important priority, more than the business, the job or the church.

- **Learn to communicate effectively.**

  Again, one of the greatest problems in the family is the lack of communication, especially from the man. I believe we have to learn to communicate effectively and be good listeners, too. If we desire to have strong family units, it is essential to maintain the lines of communication open with our spouse and children.

- **Be attentive to small details.**

  Small details keep love alive in the home. What are those small details? It could be flowers given to your wife, perhaps a small gift to your husband, an invitation to go out somewhere, a surprise birthday party, cooking your family's favorite meal, a phone call to just say "I love you", or waking your spouse with a kiss. There are many small gestures we can practice doing for our loved ones. This way the fire will be kept alive and our home will be healthy and victorious.

- **Teach your children to fear God.**

  "[6]And these words which I command you today shall be in your heart. [7]You shall teach them diligently to your children, and shall talk of them when you sit in your house, when you walk by the way, when you lie down, and when you rise up. [8]You shall bind them as a sign on your hand, and they shall be as frontlets between your eyes. [9]You shall write them on the doorposts of your house and on your gates." Deuteronomy 6.6-9

  As leaders, the best legacy we can leave our children is a **spiritual inheritance**. We can leave them money, provide for their schooling or business, but the best inheritance we can leave them is a spiritual inheritance, which is eternal. Although it is important that we leave our family a material inheritance, it is more important to leave a spiritual one, because this one lasts forever.

A few suggestions how to leave a spiritual legacy to our children are:

- We should invest money so our children can go to Christian schools. Sometimes it becomes very difficult to finance it but we should look at it as a life long investment that, in time, will bear fruit in our children, their character and personality.

- Dedicate time on a weekly or daily basis to teach them the Word of God.

  Clearly, throughout Scripture, we see how a mother and father should teach their children the biblical commandments. If our children are a priority in our lives and our desire is to leave them a legacy here on earth when we die, we must invest in quality time, teach them the Word of God and pray with them.

- Our children should go to church and worship God with us.

As long as our children are under our roof and responsibility, they must submit and obey the law of the house. One thing that should be established in the home is to set aside a day in the week to go to church together with the family, to praise and worship God. Our children will learn this and when they become adults, they too, will want to continue the example set before them by their parents. They will be honest, live in integrity and holiness; they will fear God.

"6Train up a child in the way he should go, and when he is old he will not depart from it." Proverbs 22.6

We have studied the first two priorities of a leader: his relationship and communion with God and his priority with his family. These are essential and should consume most of our time. Let us go on to the next priority.

3. The church.

Once we have fulfilled the first two priorities, we should attend and serve in the local church. I find that many leaders spend most of their time serving and helping at church, but their homes are in turmoil. They spend little or no time with their families. When a leader doesn't give his family priority in his life, then, God is not first in his life either. This is an extreme behavior that affects other priorities. Going to church is a necessity, but it can't be our number one priority. God's desire is that we fellowship and attend church regularly to praise and worship together with our brothers and sisters in harmony. When this happens, God sends His blessings.

"1Behold, how good and how pleasant it is for brethren to dwell together in unity! 2It is like the precious oil upon the head, running down on the beard, the beard of Aaron, running down on the edge of his garments." Psalms 133.1,2

Another reason we should attend a local church is because the Word tells us to serve God in His house as we serve our brothers. I believe that if a balance is maintained between priorities, (God, family and the church) the leader will be successful. It is possible to have a balanced life! I have also seen the other extreme. People that only dedicate their time and life to their family and set aside the things of God. We need to learn to set our priorities in order and do with each one as the Lord teaches us to do.

4. **The job.**

"[19]In the sweat of your face you shall eat bread till you return to the ground, for out of it you were taken; for dust you are, and to dust you shall return." Genesis 3.19

The job should be the fourth priority. After we've spent time in communion with God, after quality time is given to the family, and after we attend and serve in the church, the next thing should be our job. It is very important to keep these priorities in order. Unfortunately, many leaders commit adultery, have broken homes and their children are rebellious. This happens because there was no one to teach them, according to the Word of God, what their priorities are and in what order they should be.

CHAPTER X

Biblical Principles of a Leader

During the years in ministry and service to the Lord, I have become aware of the great shortage of leaders with principles and biblical values. Integrity is in great demand. It is time for a new generation to rise up and bring back these values and principles to this world, and lead the people to be pleasing unto the Lord. We must raise leaders to be examples in our nation, community and our families. We can be in agreement with the vision, but if the values are different, then we can't walk together.

What is a principle?

It is a divine guideline; an understanding of eternal values. It is to act accordingly in order to be successful in life. **A principle is a divine guideline directing us to make decisions based on eternal things**; it helps us be successful in life. However, a principle is not only a guideline, it is also an understanding of how we should conduct ourselves through life and what proper actions we should take based on eternal things and principles. We are the products of our own decisions. Whatever we decide today, we will be tomorrow. If you, as a leader, decide something today, it should be based on divine principles. If you do this, you will be victorious. Leaders never make decisions based on a temporary perception of things, but on biblical principles based on eternal perspectives. Every decision a leader makes today will affect his future, as well as the future of those who follow after him. Many leaders love God, but don't know how to handle themselves or how to act in certain circumstances, due to lack of knowledge. This is the reason we need to understand eternal principles; they help us to avoid failure and be successful.

Every divine principle that leads to success comes from the Word of God.

Eternal biblical principles:

1. **The principle of growing through offenses.**

   "[1]Then He said to the disciples, 'It is impossible that no offenses should come, but woe to him through whom they do come!'" Luke *17.1*

   The word **"offense"** is the Greek word *"skandalon,"* meaning trap, bait or stumbling block. It is also the name of an instrument that was used as bait to trap animals. Every time someone hurts us, we must understand that it is the enemy's trap, bait, or the hook he will use to make us stumble and fall. When we understand the true meaning of this principle, as God's leaders, and with the help of the Lord, we will be able to use these offenses to our advantage in order to grow spiritually. Learn how to forgive, apply this principle in your life and adopt it as your way of living. **For the most part, offenses come when you don't feel you are appreciated.** When a person has been serving behind the scenes, after a period of time he expects that someone would thank him, that his leader would affirm him or that someone would recognize his efforts. When this does not happen, many feel offended and stumble. There was a minister of the Gospel that was used greatly by God in the area of healing and miracles. This minister preached in a church that gave him $25.00 dollars as an offering. Later on, he went to preach at another church and again he was given $25.00 dollars as an offering. He was so disillusioned by this that he said: "If this is what it means to preach the Gospel, then I will stop preaching it." He walked away from the ministry offended because he believed the offerings did not show adequate appreciation for his service.

For the most part, people who leave ministries, the Lord or the church, are believers who were wounded in a specific area.

There is no excuse for feeling offended when we are in God's presence; there is no valid excuse. Jesus is our perfect example. We must learn to grow through every offense. Why are offenses necessary? Because they help us grow spiritually.

"7Woe to the world because of offenses! For offenses must come, but woe to that man by whom the offense comes!" Matthew 18.7

Jesus said offenses were necessary, not that God sends them, but He does use them to help us mature spiritually. As leaders of the twenty-first century, we must never forget this principle of maturity and growth through offenses. We must learn to forgive regardless of what people do to us.

How to deal with offenses:

We will learn to deal with offenses if we forgive immediately after the offense. David learned to do this a long time ago; he was quick to forgive and to ask for forgiveness. All of us need to have this same attitude towards those who offend us. If you know how to forgive, then you will be successful. Forgiving will become a way of life and an eternal value that will lead you to be a successful, spiritual leader. It is through these offenses that the spirit of Judas comes into a ministry or an organization. Judas' physical sin was to betray Jesus, his friend. Why? Because his main problem or the root of it was his disappointment due to his unfulfilled personal ambitions. Judas thought and said, "I have been with this man for three and a half years, I left my family, my home, and personal belongings to serve Him day and night. Now it seems He is not going to come through on His promises because all He talks about is His death." Realizing this, he said, "Since I am not going to get anything from Him, the least I can look forward to is selling him for 30 silver coins. After all, I deserve them for my service and sacrifice." First, the enemy spreads the spirit of Judas in the leadership. For example, people will feel discouraged and offended, thinking they are not appreciated, perhaps because they were overlooked for a promotion, not given the proper recognition or placed in the right position. These take them to self-justification until they eventually betray their leaders and sell their friends for their own gain. If you are offended, then you must learn the principle of growing through offenses. If you are overlooked, you need not lose heart, for the Lord knows everything. He makes sure justice is served when people treat you unfairly. Remember the principle of growing through offenses, forgiving as a way of life and everything will go well with you.

2. **The principle of sowing and reaping.**

"[7]Do not be deceived, God is not mocked; for whatever a man sows, that he will also reap." Galatians 6.7

This principle will either determine our success or turn us into mediocre people. We are the by-products of everything we sow. As leaders, we should keep this concept in mind. If you sow what is good, you will reap what is good. If you sow what is bad, you will reap what is bad. This principle works for those who are good, bad, fair or unjust, rich or poor, black or white. This principle has eternal results, yet many complain about what they are reaping. You must ask yourself the following questions: What have you been sowing? What have you been reaping? Is it hate, financial poverty, indifference, rejection, unforgiveness or betrayal? In simple terms, take a look at what you are sowing. If your desire is to harvest love, then you must sow love. Stop saying, "Nobody loves me," especially if you are not loving other people. If you want to reap money, then you must sow money. If your desire is to reap much, then you must sow much. This eternal principle must be applied to your life.

"[6]But this I say: He who sows sparingly will also reap sparingly, and he who sows bountifully will also reap bountifully. [7]So let each one give as he purposes in his heart, not grudgingly or of necessity; for God loves a cheerful giver." 2 Corinthians 9.6,7

This same principle works with God. He said, "If you complain and murmur about Me, then I will treat you the same way." If we desire God's blessings, we must love and praise Him. Our complaining must end. Otherwise, He will treat us the same way. Many people get tired of doing what is right because they have yet to see immediate results, but keep in mind that God never lies and His Word says, "Everything man sows, he shall reap."

"[9]And let us not grow weary while doing good, for in due season we shall reap if we do not lose heart." Galatians 6.9

The key word here is that **in due season**, we will reap what we sow. Although it might seem like we are sowing in vain, we must still apply the principle to obtain eternal results.

3. **The principle of: "Judge not, lest you be judged."**

"[1]Judge not, that you be not judged. [2]For with what judgment you judge, you will be judged; and with the measure you use, it will be measured back to you." Matthew 7.1, 2

This is one of the great principles by which we should all govern our lives. Unfortunately, many leaders fall into the sin of judgment against others. We must know that when we judge others, we are truly condemning ourselves. Personally, I have been judged and criticized, yet, I have never defended myself or answered back because I understand this principle.

What does it mean to judge?

It is the Greek word "*krino,*" meaning to separate, select, elect, to determine the sentence or to pronounce judgment.

The uses of this word in the New Testament are as follows:

- Assume the office of a judge
- Pronounce a sentence
- Condemn
- Criticize
- Execute judgment over someone else
- To form an opinion

Every time we judge someone else, we are taking over the office of judge and pronouncing sentence upon someone else. When we judge, we are criticizing and executing judgment upon another individual. We are giving the final answer, forming an opinion, and making distinction and judgment. Sometimes we might ask ourselves: Why do people judge me, saying I am a weak, fearful leader? Why are they saying I am proud and arrogant or that I am a leader who loves money? You must ask yourself if at any time, you have judged other people with these same words. With the same rod you measure, you will be measured; this is the reason you are now condemned. If people form an opinion of you, perhaps it is because you have judged others, too. Many times we judge people, organizations, nations, ethnic races, employers, pastors and family members, using phrases of self-justification to hide our judgment. For example, "I never say anything about that person, but he is rejecting me." We hide under constructive criticism to judge others. "It's not that I am judging you, but…" We want to ease our conscience before criticizing and condemning. We pass judgment left and right, without realizing we are really condemning ourselves.

What are the consequences of judging others?

- **You condemn yourself.**

"[1]Therefore you are inexcusable, O man, whoever you are who judge, for in whatever you judge another you condemn yourself; for you who judge practice the same things." Romans 2.1

The verdict is that you will become what you judge. If you judge someone for his arrogance, you will become arrogant. This also includes that people will criticize and pass judgement against us for judging.

- **You will become a stumbling block for your brother.**

"[13]Therefore let us not judge one another anymore, but rather resolve this, not to put a stumbling block or a cause to fall in our brother's way." Romans 14.13

Each time you pass judgement, a weaker brother in the faith may hear you. At this moment, you become the stumbling block for that brother who is new in the faith, causing him to fall away. For the most part, you judge in the areas in which you are weak.

- **God will judge you.**

"[3]And do you think this, O man, you who judge those practicing such things, and doing the same, that you will escape the judgment of God?" Romans 2.3

When God judges, it is a terrible, shameful thing because He does it in public. He gives us time and space to repent, but if we continue to take the position of passing judgement against our brothers, He will judge us for it. We need to live and apply this principle. We should be divine guides with eternal values, teaching people how to treat others, how to bless them and not judge them, even when it is obvious that they are in sin. Our position is not to judge, form an opinion or execute judgment.

How to stop ourselves from judging others:

- You must ask God to forgive you of your sin and repent from having passed judgment against the pastor, leader, brother, or spouse. You must ask forgiveness in God's presence, not only to Him, but also to the people you judged.
- You need to make the decision never to judge. Decide with all your heart not to criticize, condemn or judge others.
- Your decisions need to be based on divine principles; this ensures your success in this life and the one to come. Forgive those who offend you, doing what is right, and the rewards will be good. Make every decision based on eternal perspectives, not only on temporary, earthly things. Keep in mind that anything material is temporary, but the spiritual is eternal.

The following is a list of basic principles for leaders, in addition to those previously mentioned:

1. **Submission.** The leader's authority depends on his submission. A leader that is unable to submit, can't exert any authority on anyone. Submission is humility, expressed through love and service. Therefore, it is an eternal attitude. Obedience is an external attitude. This means, it is impossible to obey without submission.

2. **Character.** The basis of a leader is character. If the leader doesn't have a solid character based on integrity and honesty, then everything he builds will lack foundation; it will inevitably fall. A person's character rises to the surface when it is under pressure. But what is character? It is the behavior of an individual when he is under pressure. Character is the foundation upon which a person's morals are based.

3. **The Word and the power of God.** These are the leader's tools. Every leader must be aware that without these weapons, he is unable to accomplish anything.

4. **Sacrifice.** The way to measure the leader's success is through his sacrifice. Leaders can't be successful without paying a high price. Success can't be sold at bargain prices. Sacrifices must be made to achieve what we desire.

5. **Spiritual maturity.** Every leader must understand that to grow in spirit, soul and body is a priority. Spiritual growth must be well-rounded in every area, including one's personal life, home life, social life, education, ministry, finances and marriage.

6. **The message**. The leader's message should be **Christ crucified.** Every leader must recognize that he needs to preach about Jesus; His sacrifice, death and resurrection. This is the only message that changes the human being forever.

7. **Service.** It is the leader's nature to serve. The word **"minister"** means one who serves the people. Leaders understand that they are servants to the people. God is more interested in our availability, than our ability to serve Him.

8. **Giving.** The leader's success is found in his ability to give and not in his love of **money.** When a leader is a giver and his love of money is non-existent, God pours His blessings upon him, giving him more. God wants to prosper us financially; therefore, we can't allow the love of money to take root in our hearts, instead of God.

9. **Love.** The motivation and intention of every leader must be love. He must love everything he does, and do everything because he loves God and those around him.

10. **Marriage and family**. A leader must place great emphasis on his marriage. He should take care of his family and marriage; these should be the number one priority in his life, after God. We need to listen to our heart when making important decisions based on earthly and eternal things.

11. **The leader's role model must be Jesus.** Jesus was, and always will be, the only being who is one hundred percent God, and one hundred percent man. Therefore, He was, is, and will be, the perfect example to follow for every generation; He is the model worthy to imitate.

Do not compromise principles.

This is the story of three Hebrew men that were sent to worship other gods, such as the statue of King Nebuchadnezzar. Regardless of the fact that they would be imprisoned for life, they refused to compromise their beliefs. Even when King Nebuchadnezzar gave them their last chance to repent and save their lives, they still refused.

"[15]Now if you are ready at the time you hear the sound of the horn, flute, harp, lyre, and psaltery, in symphony with all kinds of music, and you fall down and worship the image which I have made, good! But if you do not worship, you shall be cast immediately into the midst of a burning fiery furnace. And who is the god who will deliver you from my hands?" [16]Shadrach, Meshach, and Abed-Nego answered and said to the king, "O Nebuchadnezzar, we have no need to answer you in this matter. [17]If that is the case, our God whom we serve is able to deliver us from the burning fiery furnace, and He will deliver us from your hand, O king. [18]But if not, let it be known to you, O king, that we do not serve your gods, nor will we worship the gold image, which you have set up." Daniel 3.15-18

These men were thrown into the fiery furnace and none suffered injuries. This surprised the king.

"[25]'Look!' he answered, 'I see four men loose, walking in the midst of the fire; and they are not hurt, and the form of the fourth is like the Son of God.' [26] Then Nebuchadnezzar went near the mouth of the burning fiery furnace and spoke, saying, 'Shadrach, Meshach, and Abed-Nego, servants of the Most High God, come out, and come here.' Then Shadrach, Meshach, and Abed-Nego came from the midst of the fire. [27]And the satraps, administrators, governors, and the king's counselors gathered

together, and they saw these men on whose bodies the fire had no power; the hair of their head was not singed nor were their garments affected, and the smell of fire was not on them. 28Nebuchadnezzar spoke, saying, 'Blessed be the God of Shadrach, Meshach, and Abed-Nego, who sent His Angel and delivered His servants who trusted in Him, and they have frustrated the king's word, and yielded their bodies, that they should not serve nor worship any god except their own God! 29Therefore I make a decree that any people, nation, or language which speaks anything amiss against the God of Shadrach, Meshach, and Abed-Nego shall be cut in pieces, and their houses shall be made an ash heap; because there is no other God who can deliver like this.' 30Then the king promoted Shadrach, Meshach, and Abed-Nego in the province of Babylon." Daniel 3.25-30

From this biblical passage, we can conclude several things: When a man or woman uses solid biblical principles to guide their lives, regardless of any peer pressure or temptation to compromise, yet they still continue to trust in God, it is at that moment that God blesses them. When we choose not to compromise our beliefs, the Lord gives us His protection, presence, promotion and power. Many leaders seek money, recognition and favor when they compromise their beliefs. Never do this. Remain faithful to your beliefs of honesty, integrity and transparency; God will reward you.

We must keep in mind the following when identifying the importance of a principle, or when we do something with a specific method.

- Principles are few, but methods are many.
- Principles never change; methods are always changing.
- We can't adopt a method until the principle it is based upon is understood.

To sum up everything we have learned, we could say that to develop a business, ministry, home, job, or anything else, it must be based upon a divine principle.

The following are a few questions we should ask ourselves concerning our beliefs and what could happen if we are tempted.

1. Am I capable of slandering a co-worker for a promotion?
2. Am I willing to leave my spouse for a younger, more attractive person?
3. Would I compromise my beliefs for a million dollars?
4. Am I willing to use whatever method necessary in order to accumulate money and achieve what I want?
5. Am I willing to exchange my ministry for fame?
6. Am I loyal, even in the most difficult situations?

CHAPTER XI

Values of a Leader

One reason families break up, churches are divided and organizations don't prosper is the lack of biblical values in society. Today, our society is missing biblical values; there is no morality. It is okay to lie, steal and commit fraud; good is called evil and evil is called good. There are no moral values setting limits by which people can live on a daily basis. Society is missing a good foundation on which they can build their lives.

What is a moral value? It is a biblical belief we practice daily. A sense of destiny can be derived from a moral value. Every leader has values that go hand in hand with his destiny. If we desire to know someone's destiny, we can ask ourselves what his values are. **A value is something we decide to do in a specific situation. It is not something you decide to do, without regard to circumstances, and not something based upon external pressures.** People who know what their destiny and purpose in life is, and what the will of God is for their lives, will have and practice moral values and beliefs every day until they reach the goal set by God for their lives.

Moral values of a leader:

1. **Thankfulness.**

   "28Therefore, since we are receiving a kingdom which cannot be shaken, let us have grace, by which we may serve God acceptably with reverence and godly fear." Hebrews 12.28

   The Word of God teaches that we serve God out of a thankful heart. Gratitude is part of a leader's set of values. I am grateful every day for my leaders, my family, the people and above all, God. We should always be thankful to Him. One characteristic of evil men nowadays, is their ungratefulness; they are lovers of themselves; individuals who believe they deserve everything. This should not be the attitude of the leader in this century. The attitude of every good leader should be one of gratitude towards every one.

When should we give thanks or be grateful?

- Always and for everything.

  "18In everything give thanks; for this is the will of God in Christ Jesus for you." 1 Thessalonians 5.18

  "20Giving thanks always for all things to God the Father in the name of our Lord Jesus Christ." Ephesians 5.20

Practice this moral value; make it a part of your life. Give thanks to your leaders, to your spouse and everybody who has done something for you. Surprise them with a gift as a sign of appreciation.

Bitterness makes us forget the good things and the favors others have done for us.

2. **Service.**

"7But made Himself of no reputation, taking the form of a bondservant, and coming in the likeness of men." Philippians 2.7

The leader's nature is to be a servant. The principle of how to walk on this earth was established by Jesus when He came to serve and not to be served. This principle should be a belief we carry within us. It should be practiced with our children, our spouse, our co-workers and our brothers in the faith.

How should you serve others?

- With your gifts and talents. God gives us abilities to be used in service of others.
- With your money; helping the needy. You have the ability to serve people with the financial resources God gives you.
- With your prayers. One way you can serve the people is through your prayers.

Remember to practice this value every day. Serve somebody, and whenever possible, serve those who are unable to repay you.

3. Always honor and respect authority.

"[17]Let the elders who rule well be counted worthy of double honor, especially those who labor in the word and doctrine." 1 Timothy 5.17

"[1]Let as many bondservants as are under the yoke count their own masters worthy of all honor, so that the name of God and His doctrine may not be blasphemed." 1 Timothy 6.1

The word **"honor"** means to give someone the recognition he deserves; it doesn't mean to idolize, exalt or worship him. It means to honor, respect, bless and give him his proper place. We should also pray, serve and honor him financially. We should be accountable to him and anyone who is above us in authority. One of the most important values of a leader is to know how to honor and respect his superiors, to submit to them, to honor the pastor, leader, or employer, not to question them or dispute their orders. The leader should never make any decisions without his superior's consent. Always honor his authority. If your desire is to go far in the Lord, then you must always honor his authority. For example, in the home, God is first, then the spouse. In the church, the pastor and leaders are first. At the workplace, the boss is first. Never resist authority.

4. **Always be on time for your appointments.**

"[2]He who walks uprightly, and works righteousness, and speaks the truth in his heart." Psalms 15.2

Integrity means to be unified in words and action. This means that when you promise with your mouth to be there at 5:00 p.m., you should be there at 5:00 p.m.; otherwise, it is lack of integrity on your part. If you desire this value to be part of your life, then you must practice it and be an example to others.

5. **Work as a team.**

I have leaders in my church that love and support the vision, they love my family and me, but when the moment comes to serve as a team, they fail. These leaders don't like to work as a team, but they are undergoing the learning process. This needs to be a value in our lives in order to serve God effectively. John Maxwell said in one of his laws about teamwork, "I am too small to do great things." To work as a team, it requires having values that don't exalt the ego, but gives credit to others. It recognizes the gifts in an individual and it doesn't disregard the gifts in others thinking our gift is better than theirs. We are part of a team; our only desire is to give God the glory. An example of a value we practice in our ministry is to love the people. If one person doesn't practice this value, he is unable to serve and be part of the team.

Do what you promise to do.

"[37]But let your "Yes' be "Yes,' and your "No,' "No.' For whatever is more than these is from the evil one." Matthew 5.37

Many leaders find themselves in difficulty because they lack the ability to say no. They have such a good heart, they say yes to everything. This results in the inability to finish what they promise, harming our credibility as leaders. Followers begin to see the inconsistency between our words and our actions, causing new believers to stumble. Make every effort to do what you promise you are going to do. Whether it is to God, your family or the leadership; this produces trust. If there is a possibility that we won't be able to accomplish what we promise, then we should not commit ourselves to anything. Learn to say no, even if it causes people to reject you or to lose friendships. Don't be afraid to say no; always tell the truth. We should practice this value every day. Leaders who inspire trust in people and who have followers, are those who do what they promise to do. They are not like some politicians who make many promises, but never see them through.

Affirm the people around you.

"[9]Do not be carried about with various and strange doctrines. For it is good that the heart be established by grace, not with foods which have not profited those who have been occupied with them." Hebrews 13.9

God affirms us Himself. After going through a difficult situation, we are able to hear the love of God saying to us, "I am with you; don't dismay. I will always protect and take care of you. Be strong and courageous." God is constantly affirming His people. The next verse says, "It is a good thing to affirm the heart with grace." A very important value for the leader is to always affirm the people around him. They should always be encouraged, affirmed in their identity, in their calling and job, not only in private, but in public as well. This makes people want to be around us. Affirm them! Affirm them! Affirm them!

Why should we affirm the people around us?

According to the Word of God, affirmation produces four things in the heart:

- Affirmation dignifies the individual.

  "[9]Do not be carried about with various and strange doctrines. For it is good that the heart be established by grace, not with foods which have not profited those who have been occupied with them." Hebrews13.9

  The word **"established"** means to dignify. If a person is acknowledged for his efforts, it dignifies him as a person and raises his self-esteem.

- Affirmation establishes.

  When we affirm someone around us, what we are really doing is establishing that person, helping him to be well rooted, to be stronger in God, to be validated in his identity and heart, to be edified on solid ground, to trust more in God, and so forth.

- Affirmation strengthens.

  It would be a good thing for you to test this out on people around you. If these people feel discouraged and weak, and you offer words of affirmation, this will establish and dignify them. After you validate them for a job well done, you will immediately see them strengthened in their calling and in their identity in God.

- Affirmation makes the person feel secure.

  The same word "established" in Hebrews 13.9 says, "For it is good for the heart to be established and ennobled and strengthened by means of grace," (Amplified Bible). There are many potential leaders waiting to be assured by a father or mentor. They lack direction and wonder if what they are doing is the right thing. They are also unsure of their calling and the decisions they must make. They need a father to affirm, validate and confirm that the decision they are about to make is the right one. To affirm, establish, acknowledge, strengthen and assure the heart of people, should always be a value in our leaders; an art they should practice daily.

8. Always have a positive attitude.

An attitude can destroy or lift the morale in a team. It is possible for a person with a lousy attitude to become the "rotten apple" and contaminate the whole team. Attitude is an internal disposition of the heart; we face life with it. It is a decision of the heart. We decide if we are going to be happy or sad, angry or at peace. There are no excuses for having a bad attitude. Stop saying, "My husband made me like this" or "The devil made me do it." You decide to be angry or not. Good or bad attitudes are decisions of the heart. As a pastor, I decided to have a positive attitude a long time ago, without regards to what is happening around me, or what pressure I am under. If I am going through a crisis, I try to have a positive attitude, because it is up to me what attitude I am going to have through any given circumstance. This is one of my greatest attributes, one I practice when I am at the office, with my family or with the leadership. I choose to have a victorious attitude.

9. Be a peacemaker.

A peacemaker puts an end to disagreements between two parties, extinguishing fires instead of igniting them. He ends division and gossip, and is always seeking to create a peaceful atmosphere. To be a peacemaker is an attribute of every good leader; this is to say, he seeks peace at all times, and he doesn't look for fights, but if there are any, he puts an end to them.

10. Always give the glory to God.

"11 You are worthy, O Lord, to receive glory and honor and power; for

You created all things, and by Your will they exist and were created." Revelation 4.11

This is another attribute I practice, giving glory to God in everything, not only in private, but in public. As leaders, we need to teach our leadership and the people to recognize that God is great, He is marvelous, and His grace and favor bless and prosper us. What we are and what we have is because of His grace and mercy. As a pastor, I always teach the people the most important value to practice every day is to give the glory to God for the victories, prosperity, and His signs and wonders. We can never rob Him of His glory because the day we do it, will be the day His anointing upon us will end. Every time we achieve a victory in any area of our lives, we must give God the recognition for that victory. We must acknowledge it in private and in public. It must be established that it was not by our human strength, but by His power.

"[6]So he answered and said to me: "This is the word of the LORD to Zerubbabel: Not by might nor by power, but by My Spirit,' Says the LORD of hosts." Zechariah 4.6

In everything I do, (a letter, pamphlet, announcement for the television, radio, commercial, teaching, class, preaching, sermon, book or article), I make sure the name of Jesus is exalted and not the name of the pastor or ministry. Our biblical value is always to exalt and give Him the glory. After every victory, we must recognize what the Lord gives us, in front of the congregation.

11. Seek unity among the brothers.

"[3]Endeavoring to keep the unity of the Spirit in the bond of peace." Ephesians 4.3

One thing that makes the corporate anointing descend upon our lives and congregation is harmony and unity. I love unity with all my heart and I always make every effort to safeguard it and promote it among the brethren. The opposite of seeking unity is planting disagreements among the people. This is one of the greatest sins God hates.

"[19]A false witness who speaks lies, and one who sows discord among brethren." Proverbs 6.19

A person who sows division is one who gossips instead of ending the disagreement. He listens to the gossip and spreads it. As a result, he fights and causes great division. An attribute a great leader is to seek peace and unity among the brethren, his friends, family members and even with his enemies.

12. Be accountable to someone.

"[21]Submitting to one another in the fear of God." Ephesians 5.21

We should all be accountable to someone above us, regardless of how high we have risen or how deep we have gone.

Why should we be accountable to others?

- *For our own protection*. We all have weak areas; we make mistakes and commit errors. Sometimes we don't have leaders around us with the strength to discipline or correct us. This is the reason we should have a mentor, a spiritual father, a covering, someone we can open our hearts to and who will help us in our weak moments. A pastor or leader can't go to his sheep for counseling; it could cause them to stumble and fall. He should always look for someone with greater authority than him.

- *To be disciplined*. We all limp in at least one specific area of our lives. When we make a mistake, we need someone with greater anointing and authority to discipline and rebuke us. I am not saying God won't use other people to make adjustments or to shake us up a bit. Of course He will, but we should always have someone above us in authority to whom we can be accountable. I have a mentor and I, voluntarily, hold myself accountable to him regarding my family, the church, money and the vision. Why do I do this? For my own protection and to be corrected.

- *When we are accountable for our actions, the people feel safe*. As leaders, we are constantly reminding the people to submit, to be obedient to us, but the people, when they are required to do this, the first thing they ask is, "And my leader, to whom is he accountable? To whom does he submit to?" If they find you are accountable to someone higher than you are and that you don't go around doing whatever pleases you, but you hold yourself accountable, then it helps them to feel secure. An attribute we should always practice in the home, in our business, at our workplace or in our nation, should be accountability. If we do this, we will be protected, and when we are disciplined, the people will feel more secure.

13. Be transparent.

"[8]Therefore let us keep the feast, not with old leaven, nor with the leaven of malice and wickedness, but with the unleavened bread of ***sincerity*** *and truth." 1 Corinthians 5.8*

The synonym for the word transparency is **sincerity**. In the Greek language, this is the word *"eilikrineia,"* meaning purity or transparency. It also means to be judged in the light of day. The word is derived from the bazaars in the Orient where the pottery was exhibited in dimly lit rooms. The unscrupulous merchants would mend the broken vases by covering their cracks with wax. Intelligent buyers would hold these vases high, exposing them to the sun's light to judge their quality. The word "*eilikreneia*" means honesty, transparency, genuine purity or uncontaminated innocence. A transparent person is someone who evaluates his motives and intentions, and finds he has nothing to hide. An extremely important attribute for a leader to have is to be transparent before God, his family, the people, in his business, with his leaders; to be pure, genuine, without deception and sincere every day of his life. It is when we have no defects (cracks) we must cover up and when we are no longer in need of a mask to hide our hypocrisy. On the contrary, we should be the same in public as in private. An attribute in my life has been to always judge the motives and intentions of my heart before doing anything. Every time I get ready to do anything in my life, I ask myself certain questions. For example:

- Am I dong this in Jesus' name?

  "17And whatever you do in word or deed, do all in the name of the Lord Jesus, giving thanks to God the Father through Him." Colossians 3.17

  Do everything in the name of Jesus.

- Am I doing this with all my heart?

  Every time we do something for God, it should be done with all our heart.

  "23And whatever you do, do it heartily, as to the Lord and not to men." Colossians 3.23

- Am I doing this for the glory of God?

  Before doing something, ask yourself if this is for your own benefit or to exalt your own name. Is it to exalt your business or ministry, or is it for the glory of God, that Jesus' name may be exalted. Let us practice the attributes of being transparent, judging our own motives and intentions in the light of the Word, and being genuine and without hypocrisy. The people are tired of seeing so many hypocritical leaders; they need sincere, transparent role models. We need to keep in mind that some day we will be judged for the motives and intentions of our heart.

14. We should be radical worshippers.

"[23]But the hour is coming, and now is, when the true worshipers will worship the Father in spirit and truth; for the Father is seeking such to worship Him. [24]God is Spirit, and those who worship Him must worship in spirit and truth." John 4.23, 24

I practice this attribute every day, not only when I am at church, but at home, in my office, when I am sad or happy, when I wake up or go to sleep, when the sun rises in the morning or at sunset. I worship Him, even when I am going through difficult times; I practice this belief every day. I praise and worship God all the time! Many people ask themselves why David's heart was pleasing to God. There are three characteristics that made David's heart pleasing and great before God:

- David was quick in humbling himself and repenting for his sin. Every time he offended the Lord, he immediately recognized his downfall and humbly repented.

- David was a warrior. The Word calls David a "man of war" and his heart was created for it. He fought to establish the kingdom of God.

- David was a worshipper. Every time we read the Scriptures, we see David adoring and worshipping God. This was an attribute, a belief he practiced daily.

Murmuring and complaining extends our misery and our problems, but worshipping God ends them.

15. Take care of our physical body.

"[19]Or do you not know that your body is the temple of the Holy Spirit who is in you, whom you have from God, and you are not your own?" 1 Corinthians 6.19

Physical exercise is part of my routine during the week. I believe this to be an attribute few leaders practice, perhaps because they don't have the time, others because they simply don't feel like it. This is an attribute we have to decide to do because our body is the temple of the Holy Spirit and it must be taken care of. Physical exercise is not meant to make us better athletes, but to keep us in shape and to give us more energy to serve God. The Lord created the body to be healthy. We should commit ourselves to eat a healthy diet. We need to avoid eating the things that damage our health, such as greasy and canned foods, sodas and n general all kinds of junk food. The only thing these types of food are good for is depleting us of our energy and making us sick.

What must we do to take care of our physical body?

We must learn to be self-disciplined with physical exercise, take time to rest, take a vacation once in a while and watch what we eat. Don't put in your mouth everything that is offered to you. Be disciplined; maintain this as an important attribute in your life.

16. A good relationship with God.

"[14]The secret of the LORD is with those who fear Him, and He will show them His covenant." Psalms 25.14

It is a priority, important and essential for every leader to have a close relationship with God. It implies seeking His face, adoring Him, reading His Word, meditating on it, praying each day, and having a close, permanent relationship with Him.

17. Think before you act.

"[16]Every prudent man acts with knowledge, but a fool lays open his folly." Proverbs 13.16

I believe, for the most part, many leaders make decisions based upon impulsive reactions and without thinking. One thing God's wisdom teaches is that we must think before we act, as opposed to reacting to someone else's bad attitude. When we do this, we place ourselves at their mercy. The Bible refers to thinking before acting as a wise thing to do. This is also an attribute for me. Many people offend and criticize me. My immediate, natural reaction is one of anger. At that moment, my desire is to go and give them a piece of my mind. But immediately, I take control of my anger. I wait and think about what my answer should be. When I analyze the whole scenario, calmly and peacefully, my decision is not to answer with profanity, but with blessings. This decision is the result of thinking before reacting. If I act without thinking, I would get myself into great difficulty. I have met people who react before thinking. The Bible calls them stubborn and headstrong. However, if we think things through and then act, the Word of God says, we are wise and prudent.

18. Forgiveness as a way of life.

"[25]And whenever you stand praying, if you have anything against anyone, forgive him, that your Father in heaven may also forgive you your trespasses." Mark 11.25

I decided a long time ago not to let what people do affect me. I choose to forgive them. Regardless of how often people offend me, forgiveness is, and always will be, a life style choice for me. I decided not to allow one single day to go by without forgiving those who offend me. I also decided to never hold a grudge, resentment or bitterness in my heart against anyone; this could ruin or damage my relationship with God. This also affects my physical body, it destroys my finances and it's a great impediment to receiving God's blessings. For me, this has always been an attribute; it will always be something I practice with determination.

19. Bless those who curse us.

"[44]But I say to you, love your enemies, bless those who curse you, do good to those who hate you, and pray for those who spitefully use you and persecute you." Matthew 5.44

Leaders that are doing great things for God and making an impact on nations, cities and people, will always be persecuted; many will curse them. To **"curse"** means to speak badly about someone or something. Therefore, if you are real leader, you should be accustomed to people cursing you. If we practice this attribute, (blessing those who curse you), God's blessings will always be with you. Every day, when you wake up, you should open your mouth to bless, to speak well of others and to speak well of those who curse and persecute you.

20. Confrontation.

In chapter five, we learned what confrontation means and how Jesus teaches this value as something that should be part of our way of life. It is necessary for us to wisely confront our family, our friends and those with whom we disagree and have problems. Confrontation helps us to understand our own problems and those of others.

21. Always tell the truth.

"[17]*A proud look, a lying tongue, hands that shed innocent blood." Proverbs 6.17*

God hates and detests seven sins, the root of all of them being a lying spirit. God hates a lying tongue and false witness. Unfortunately, we find there is much lying in the world today, including the church.

Telling the truth can be costly, but it is better to please God and not men. We should always tell the truth, even when we are under pressure. Even if there is a lot at stake, we should never compromise the biblical principles for a "bowl of lentils." Everything we accomplish with a lie, eventually becomes a curse. Stop lying, even if this means losing a friend, a job, a position or anything else.

There was a sister in the faith who worked as a secretary. She was fired because her boss received a phone call from his wife and he asked his secretary to lie, saying that he was not in the office, when in reality, he was in his office with his lover. The sister, who was his secretary, answered her boss, "I will not lie. I will tell your wife you are in your office, and if she asks me who you're with, I will tell her the truth." He was so angry he fired the sister. Two weeks later, she found a better job with more benefits. God honored her obedience. Although at times it might seem that we're losing, always speak the truth; God will back us up. This should be a moral virtue to every good leader. Always speak the truth, regardless of the consequences. In the long run, God will reward us and never leave us.

22. Quality time with the family.

This attribute should be practiced daily. We should spend quality time with our family. We must set time aside to pray with our children, play with them and teach them the Word of God.

23. Pray before making an important decision.

Praying continually demonstrates our dependency upon God. If we are good leaders, we should be completely dependent upon Him. Every time we need to make decisions, we should pray and consult God. Aside from the fact that this is a sign of humility and responsibility, we must keep in mind that any decision we make affects everyone around us. On many occasions, it could affect nations or the organization to which we belong. Praying before making any decisions, should be every good leader's belief.

24. Live in covenant relationships.

"[24]A man who has friends must himself be friendly, but there is a friend who sticks closer than a brother." Proverbs 18.24

I firmly believe that the last move of God upon the face of the earth, the one the Lord will bring, will be through men and women who have covenant relationships and not just through one man. Covenant relationships are made to bring people together, to work and make an impact upon the kingdom of God; not to satisfy our selfish needs. Every minister, apostle, prophet and evangelists who comes to our ministry, come because we have a covenant of friendship. Everything I desire for the ministry, or myself, I pray that they receive it. Everything they want for themselves or their ministry, they want me to have. A covenant is a mutual agreement, whereby we help each other in our personal life, our family or ministry. In a covenant relationship, we offer each other all the resources God has given us and all the tools needed to develop leaders and people. A covenant means to be faithful and loyal to each other. This includes offering to instruct the people and give words of encouragement when needed. When there is a covenant relationship everything is made available for mutual success. A covenant relationship enables us to help our brother, to encourage him and help him achieve success in God. This is an important moral virtue. We must begin to ask God, as leaders, to bring men and women to us with a kingdom and a team mentality, one that desires our success and offers us the tools needed for the people of God to grow and be prosper.

24. Life in covenant relationships.

A man who has friends must himself be friendly, but there is a friend who sticks closer than a brother. Proverbs 18:24

I firmly believe that the end move of God upon the face of the earth, the one the Lord will bring, will be through men and women who have covenant relationships and not just through one man. Covenant relationships are made to bring people together to work and make an impact upon the kingdom of God, not to satisfy our selfish needs. Every minister, apostle, prophet and evangelist who comes to our ministry come because we have a covenant of friendship. Everything I desire for the ministry, is the same thing that they desire. Everything they want for themselves in their ministry, they want me to have. A covenant is a mutual agreement, whereby we help each other in our personal lives and in our ministry. In a covenant relationship, we offer each [illegible] resources God has given us and all the tools needed to develop [illegible] and peoples. A covenant means to be faithful and loyal [illegible] other. This includes offering to instruct the people and give words of encouragement when needed. When there is a covenant relationship everything is made available for mutual success. A covenant relationship enables us to help our brother, to encourage him and help him achieve success in God. This is an important moral virtue. We must begin to ask God to lead us to bring men and women to us with a kingdom and a team mentality, one that desires our success and offers us the tools needed for the people of God to grow and be prosper.

The Sinner's Prayer

Right now, where you are sitting, if you desire to receive the greatest gift of eternal life through Jesus Christ, please accompany me in this prayer, repeat it in a loud, audible voice:

> *"Heavenly Father, I recognize that I am a sinner and that my sin separates me from you. I repent from all of my sins and confess Jesus as my Lord and Savior, of my own free will. I believe He died for my sins. I believe with all my heart that God, the Father, raised Him from the dead. Jesus, I ask you to come into my heart and change my life. I renounce all covenants with the enemy. If I die right now, when I open my eyes, I will be in your arms. Amen!*

If this prayer reflects the sincere desire of your heart, observe what Jesus said about the decision you just made:

"9 If you confess with your mouth the Lord Jesus and believe in your heart that God has raised Him from the dead, you will be saved. 10 For with the heart one believes unto righteousness, and with the mouth confession is made unto salvation." Romans 10.9, 10

"47 Most assuredly, I say to you, he who believes in Me has everlasting life." John 6.47

The Sinner's Prayer

Right now, where you are sitting, if you desire to receive the greatest gift of eternal life through Jesus Christ, please accompany me in this prayer, repeat it in a loud, audible voice:

[illegible]

If this prayer reflects the sincere desire of your heart, observe what Jesus said about the decision you just made:

"[9]*If you confess with your mouth the Lord Jesus and believe in your heart that God has raised Him from the dead, you will be saved.* [10]*For with the heart one believes unto righteousness, and with the mouth confession is made unto salvation.*" Romans 10:9,10

"[47]*Most assuredly, I say to you, he who believes in Me has everlasting life.*" John 6:47

Conclusion

The will of God for this century is to raise up men and women who know who they are, who love to serve in the kingdom of God and who desire with all their hearts to do His will. You now hold in your hands a book you can use as a guide for personal training and perhaps, someday, you might leave it as a legacy to your disciples. If you are capable of releasing what you have learned and depositing what you have received into others, then this book has accomplished its mission. The reason God inspired me to write it was to motivate you to create an army of men and women who love the Lord with all their soul, heart and strength, people willing to lay down their lives to serve their peers, enlarge the kingdom of God and take His Word throughout the world.

Bibliography

Biblia Plenitud. 1994 Caribe Editorial, Nashville, TN 37214, ISBN: 9780899222813

Dictionary Spanish to English, English to Spanish. Larousse Editorial S.A., Printed in Denmark, Num. 81, Mexico, ISBN: 2034202007, ISBN: 70607371X, 1993.

Elmore, Tim. *Soul Provider.* Published by Here's Life Publishers, Inc., San Bernardino, CA 92402, U.S.A. ISBN: 0898403448, pp. 71,75, 107-109.

Engstrom, Ted W. *Un lider no nace, se hace.* Betania Caribe Editorial, 1980, Nashville, TN. Printed in U.S.A. ISBN: 0881133302, pp. 117, 119.

Expanded Edition the Amplified Bible. Zondervan Bible Publishers. ISBN: 0310951682, 1987 – Lockman Foundation USA.

Maxwell, John. *Aprecie a las personas.* 2nd Vida Editorial, 1997. SP Publications, Inc. Printed in the U.S.A., ISBN: 0-829718621, pp. 158-160.

Maxwell, John . *Developing the Leader within You.* Betania Caribe Editorial, 1996. Printed in the U.S.A. ISBN: 08-881132934, pp. 117, 119.

Maxwell, John C. *Desarrolle el lider que esta en usted*. Betania, Caribe Editorial, 1996. Printed in the U.S.A. ISBN: 08-881132934, PP.55, 59, 169.

Maxwell, John C. *Developing leaders around you.* Thomas Nelson, 1995. ISBN: 0-840767471, pp. 127, 128.

Monroe, Myles. *Becoming a leader*. Pneuma Life, 1993. Printed in the U.S.A. ISBN: 1-56229401-6, pp. 30, 43, 44, 134, 142, 159, 158.

Monroe, Myles, *Releasing your potential*. Destiny Image Publishers, 1993. ISBN: 1-560430729, pp. 16-18.

Reiland, Dan. *Shoulder to Shoulder*. Prologue by John Maxwell. Published in Nashville, TN by Thomas Nelson Inc. Publishers, Printed in the U.S.A. ISBN: 0-785272488, pp. 130, 131.

Reina-Valera 1995 – Study Edition, (United States of America: United Biblical Societies) 1998.

Sanders, J. Oswald. *Liderazgo espiritual.* Portavoz Publishers, 1995. Printed in the U.S.A. ISBN: 0-825416507, pp. 119, 123, 125, 126.

Strong James, S.T.D., L.L.D. *Strong Exhaustive Concordance of the Bible*, Caribe Editorial, Inc., Thomas Nelson, Inc., Publishers, Nashville, TN - Miami, FL, U.S.A., 2002. ISBN: 0-89922-382-6.

Vine, W.E. *An Expository Dictionary of Old and New Testament Words.* Caribe Editorial, Inc./División Thomas Nelson, Inc., Nashville, TN, ISBN: 0899224954, 1999.

Ward, Lock A. *Nuevo Diccionario de la Biblia.* Unilit Editorial: Miami, Florida, ISBN: 0-7899-0217-6, 1999.

GM INTERNATIONAL

PRESENTS:
BOOKS THAT WILL EDIFY YOUR SPIRITUAL LIFE

Inner Healing and Deliverance
Learn how to live in victory
Also available in Spanish and in French.

The New Wine Generation
God is preparing a new generation under His Anointing and the power of the Holy Spirit
Also available in Spanish and in French.

Overcoming Depression
Making the best out of the difficult situations in our lives
Also available in Spanish.

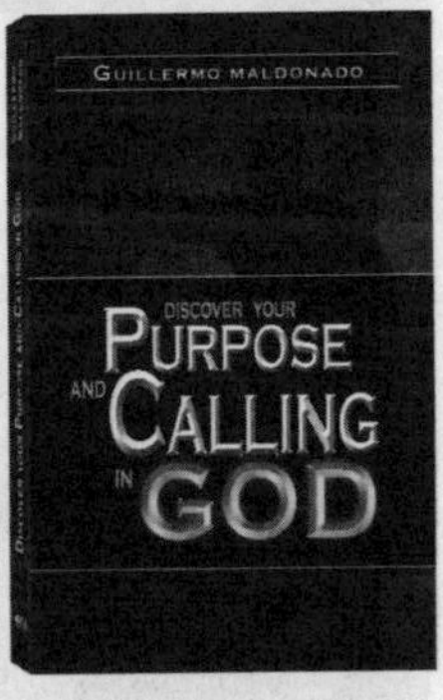

Discover your Purpose and Calling in God
Discover your spiritual gifts and your calling. Learn how to be in the perfect will of God for your life
Also available in Spanish.

Forgiveness
How to deal with offenses in a positive way
Also available in Spanish and in French.

The Holy Anointing
How to flow in the supernatural power of God's Anointing
Also available in Spanish and in French.

Call today to place your order.
Our friendly staff is ready to help with your request and will be glad to suggest the best resources you need.

You may also visit us at: www.gmministries.org
GM International Tel: 305-233-3325